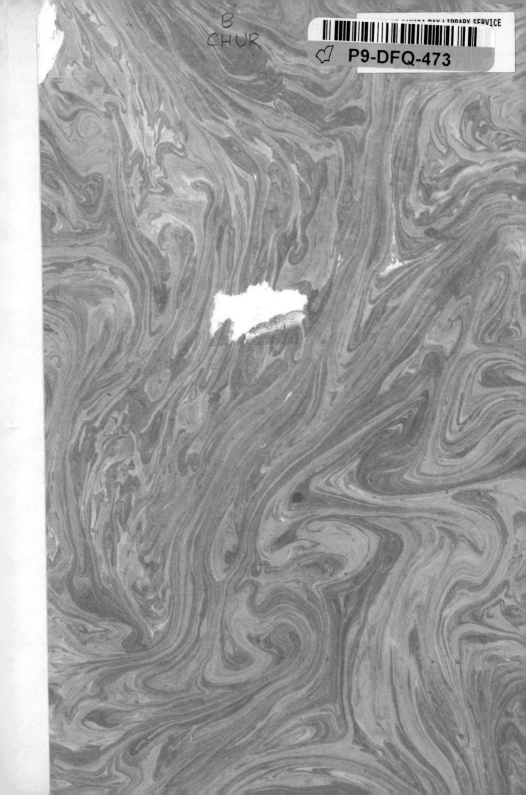

CHURCHILL

© EDIMAT BOOKS Ltd. London
is an affiliate of Edimat Libros S.A.
C/ Primavera, 35 Pol. Ind. El Malvar
Arganda del Rey - 28500 (Madrid) Spain
E-mail: edimat@edimat.es

Title: *Churchill*
In charge of the Work:
Francisco Luis Cardona Castro
Doctor in History by the Barcelona University
and Professor
Coordination of texts:
Manuel Giménez Saurina, Manuel Mas Franch
and Miguel Giménez Saurina

ISBN: 84-9794-017-2
Legal Deposit: M-48407-2004

PRINTED IN SPAIN

INTRODUCTION

How can we find adequate words to introduce somebody as great as Winston Churchill?

Born into one of England's great aristocratic families, Churchill had rather an unhappy childhood: his family was never a very close one, and he grew up without seeing much of his parents. Perhaps the solitude, forced upon him, was the reason he decided, as a young boy, that he was going to grow up to be somebody famous and important. It could be said that it was the lack of affection from his father that drove Churchill to resolve his future at such an early age: he would dedicate his life to making people sit up and take notice, and while he lived, England would be the country that he wanted it to be. His destiny was clear to him and he would not rest until it was fulfilled.

His determination certainly never failed him; during his long life he marked his progress with many great accomplishments, and although there were also some significant failures, his commitment earned him the trust of the whole country.

Soldier, writer, artist, politician, talented war strategist and noble statesman: Churchill performed them all, to be invested almost at the end of his life with the honour of knighthood. He soon developed a personal charisma that set him apart from the rest — his way of dressing, the cigars that hung permanently from his mouth, his expressive gestures and his audacious, somewhat cynical speeches made a huge impact during the twentieth century. Churchill was above all a great actor. He knew that to leave a firm impression he must not hesitate in overacting almost to the point of appearing comical.

But this great caricature of a politician was more than capable of defending his country's interests, and it could be said, those of the whole world. Without such a man, capable of standing up to Hitler, the Europe of today could have turned out to be a very different place. If Churchill had not unyieldingly refused to surrender when Great Britain stood alone against the frenzied attacks of Hitler, the Second World War may well have finished earlier, but the genocide and avarice at the hands of the German dictator may have proven unstoppable.

It has been said that Churchill did not truly understand the latest trends of his age, and also that he had no talent for conducting the economical or financial aspects of politics, but it cannot be denied that he never doubted in bringing Great Britain through the War to peace, and to what he had promised the people of his country: Victory.

Bibliography

ALESIO ROBLES, M.: *Winston Churchill,* Botas, Mexico, 1943

BALANYÁ, E. S.: *Winston Chruchill, vida de un hombre de acción,* Pace, Madrid, 1944.

BLACK, E.: *Churchill,* Grijalbo, Barcelona, 1972.

CHASTENET, J.: *Churchill y la Inglaterra del siglo XX,* Ariel, Barcelona, 1957

CHURCHILL: *Obras Escogidas,* Aguilar, Madrid, 1969.

— *Historia de los pueblos de habla inglesa,* edited by Luis de Caralt, Barcelona, 1960.

GUFFAN, J.: *Churchill,* Massin, Paris, 1978.

GUILLEMOT, P.: *Churchill,* Amigos de la Historia, Madrid, 1975.

KERNAN, R. H.: Churchill, *Biografía,* Aymá, Barcelona, 1944.

LORD MORAN: *Winston Churchill. Memorias de un médico,* edited by Taurus, Madrid, 1967.

MERTENS, Th. A.: *Churchill,* Argos-Vergara, Barcelona, 1970.

MOOREHEAD, ALAN: *Churchill,* Salvat, Barcelona, 1987.

RODRÍGUEZ LÁZARO, J.: *Winston Churchill,* Astoreca, Bilbao, 1982.

VV.AA.: *Churchill,* Urbión, Madrid, 1984.

CHAPTER I

WINSTON LEONARD CHURCHILL IS BORN

Randolph Churchill, third son of the Duke of Marlborough, met his wife-to-be at a party held in honour of the Russian Tsar and Tsarina on the Royal Yacht Ariadne.

Jeanne Jerome, as was the maiden name of Lady Randolph Churchill, came from an English family who had emigrated to the United States during the previous century. Once there, one of the sons had married the daughter of an Iroquois chief, and together they had settled in New York, where they became wealthy and prestigious among New York society. Jeanne's father succeeded in becoming the owner of the New York Times.

His wife and daughters were accustomed to spending long periods of time in Europe, and it was during one of these visits that Jeanne met Randolph Churchill. Three days after meeting her, Randolph asked for Jeanne's hand in marriage. He was twenty-four and she was nineteen. Nobody saw any reason to object and so the wedding went ahead.

The following year, on the 30th November 1874, the seventh Duke of Marlborough threw a great ball, to which professors and students at Oxford University and all the nobility of the region were invited. The ball was a great event; the men in their best formal attire; the military officers in full dress uniform; and all ladies rivalling one another in refinement.

One of the most admired ladies at the ball was the daughter-in-law of the Duke of Marlborough, Lady Jeanne Churchill. But she was seven months pregnant, and after an afternoon's foxhunting her over-enthusiastic dancing overwhelmed her, and she fainted.

Doctor Taylor, a guest at the ball, realised that she was in labour. There was no time to reach her private rooms because they were on the other side of the palace. A makeshift bed was quickly put up in one of the cloakrooms next to the ballroom, and it was there that Winston Churchill was brought into the world.

The baby endured the difficulties of being two months premature, and one month later, on 27th December, Lord and Lady Randolph Churchill's son was baptised in the palace chapel by the Duke of Marlborough's chaplain, Reverend Henry William Yule. The baby was christened Winston Leonard Spencer Churchill.

At the beginning of 1875 the Churchill family returned to their residence in Charles Street, London. Winston's father had been elected to the House of Commons for the constituency of Woodstock. Both he and his wife took pleasure in the pomp and circumstance of London society, which meant that Lady Randolph had little time to spend with her son. They employed Mrs. Everest as Winston's nanny and she took on the role of caring for the baby, at times even taking the place of his mother.

Ireland

In January, 1877, the family moved to Dublin. This came about as a result of an adultery scandal involving the Prince of Wales and Randolph's brother, Blandford Churchill. The Prince and Randolph had been good friends, but Randolph found himself obliged to take his family's side in the argu-

Winston Churchill, the wise old statesman.

ment, and his friendship with the future King Edward VII was sacrificed. The doors of London's aristocracy were closed on the Churchill family when the future King declared that he would not grace any party at which Randolph was received.

The Duke of Marlborough, who was also the Viceroy of Ireland, being well aware of his son's situation, took him off to Ireland, where he was to act as his father's private secretary.

Winston was then two years old, and the family remained in Ireland until he was five, when in March 1880, Lord and Lady Randolph had to return to London in order to prepare for the forthcoming election campaign in April.

Winston Churchill's education

Once back in London, Winston and his younger brother received instruction in reading and writing from Mrs. Everest. It was soon decided that Winston should attend school though, and in November 1881, he was enrolled as a boarder at St. George's School in Ascot. This was the start of an unhappy time for Winston, for while he was there he received hardly any visits from his parents.

It was during this time that Lord Randolph re-established his relationship with the Prince of Wales, which was to lead to a brilliant, though brief, political career, unfortunately cut short by his early death.

Winston was not an outstanding pupil, and in 1884 his parents decided to take him out of the school where he boarded and enrol him in another, also as a boarder, at Hove, near Brighton. The Thompson sisters ran the school, and Winston's studies improved there; he was much happier than he had been in the gloomy St George's.

Meanwhile, his father began to scale the political ladder, gradually making a name for himself as one of the most promising men in the Conservative Party. In 1884, his entry into the government was assured, and in 1886, he was given the prestigious post of Chancellor of the Exchequer. However, on the 20th December of the same year, Lord Randolph was to resign from the post in a difference of opinion over the drawing up of the annual military budget.

In 1887, at thirteen years old, Winston left his school in Hove to start at Harrow, a public school. At fifteen he was required to choose the direction that he wanted his studies to take, but his father made the decision for him, and obliged him to opt for a military career. Winston accepted the decision, and remained at Harrow to prepare for the entrance examination for the Sandhurst Military Academy.

Preparation was very hard and he was unable to take the examination until July of 1892. However, he failed the examination twice, once then and again when he sat for a second time a year later. After two frustrated attempts he was forced to leave Harrow.

He continued studying for the examination at the Captain James Academy, where he finally passed, although helped by the influence of the examining board. He was, after all, the son of a Duke.

CHAPTER II
THE YOUNG SOLDIER

Winston Churchill began his military career at the end of August 1893, at the Academy or Royal Military College, in Sandhurst, next to Portsmouth road, about twenty-five miles from London. Winston spent a year at the College as a military cadet, which to all appearances he enjoyed. He learnt new things and took a disciplined approach to the tough school for cavalry soldiers, and he was able to return home often on leave to stay with his family, where he could show off his red and gold cadet's dress uniform.

In his free time he made the most of the distractions available at Sandhurst and he was also known to have frequented a coffee shop in London, which boasted live music and a back room that was frequented by women of dubious reputation. When a certain woman of some social standing tried to close the bar, Churchill led a protest to keep it open. The result was that the authorities decided to keep the back room open, but separated from the rest of the establishment by a partition. Churchill used the occasion to give a speech on the virtues of liberty and tolerance.

Winston Churchill finished his studies in 1894, achieving eighth place out of one hundred and fifty degree places, and was awarded a certificate of merit. The following year he was posted to the Fourth Regiment of Hussars, with its headquarters in Aldershot.

That same year, in 1894, saw Winston's father on his death bed. The former Chancellor of the Exchequer had been suffering from a mental illness that called for complete rest, but unaware of the seriousness of his situation he insisted on continuing his political activities as normal. He was eventually persuaded to embark on a trip around the world, as it was thought that the voyage might improve his illness, but midway through the journey his health took a turn for the worse, obliging him to return to London, where he died one month later, in January, 1895.

For Winston, his father's death provoked mixed reactions. The Duke had never shown him much affection, and Winston was now free to take control of his own life, but Winston had had a great deal of respect and admiration for the man and his death affected him deeply. Years later he was to write in one of his books:

> I was resting in a nearby apartment, I ran through Grosvenor Square, getting covered with snow. It was 24th January. After a long period of confusion and unconsciousness he died without pain. My dreams of entering Parliament at his side, those dreams that united us, were over. Now I could only pursue the same goals in his memory.

The death of Lord Randolph coincided almost exactly with Winston finishing his studies at Sandhurst. He was awarded his official diploma on the 20th February 1895, having spent about two weeks in the Fourth Regiment of Hussars in Aldershot.

Life in the regiment was under the strict order of Colonel Beabazon, and proved to be much harder than that at Sandhurst. Churchill was not content to be only a mediocre officer and aspired to stand out in his regiment. Exercises on horseback were part of the daily routine, and it was during this period that Winston acquired his love for polo.

But 1895 turned out to be a fateful year for Winston, firstly for the death of his father, and then when his beloved nanny, Mrs. Everest, also passed away. She and Winston had always remained in contact through visits and writing letters.

The economic situation of the Churchill family had reached a critical point by this time. The unending series of parties that Winston's parents attended, and their long journeys in Europe and America had reduced their economic reserves practically to the point of ruin. The situation had been precarious for quite a time prior to the death of Lord Randolph, but due to the family's social position as part of the aristocracy they were obliged to maintain the lifestyle this status required.

Mrs. Everest had worked for the family since Winston's birth, first as a nanny for Winston and his brother, until they were old enough to be sent to school, and then as a housekeeper. When the financial situation had become desperate, Mrs. Everest had been given her notice. At the time of her death, Winston's mother was in Paris and did not return for the funeral. Winston however, who had always adored his nanny, hurried to be at her side when he learnt of the gravity of her illness. She died on 3rd July.

Churchill never spoke anything but praise about Mrs. Everest, and he makes many references to her in his writings. On her death, he ordered an inscription for her gravestone.

In November 1895 Winston requested a posting to Cuba to act as an observer in the political revolt developing against the government of Spain. In 1868, the deposing of Queen Isabel II of Spain (1843 - 1868) marked the beginning of what was called the *Sexenio Revolucionario* (Six Year Revolution), inspired by the Liberal ideals of independence and instigated by activists such as Maceo, Gómez and Martí, who led the

Cuban people in a separatist movement which followed on from the *Grito del Yara* (Cry of Yara). The first war lasted ten years and culminated in the *Paz de Zanjón*, a peace treaty made by General Martínez Campos, which promised the insurgents certain concessions towards independence. The peace, however, was only a temporary pause in fighting, as neither the Spanish government, King Alfonso XII being on the throne at the time, nor the Spanish Courts had ratified the treaty made by the General.

Faced with a new war situation in 1895, Martínez Campos attempted to use diplomacy rather than force to prevent the spreading of a military operations over the whole island. However, his tolerant attitude did not bear well with headquarters in Madrid, and he was replaced by Weyler, a tough Mallorcan officer of German origin, who used extreme tactics to subdue the rebels, such as the destruction of the harvests in 1896; the prohibition of tobacco exports, and the detention of Cubans in fortified villages in the form of concentration camps. The United States, which was anxious to expand its interest in the area and had supported the uprising from the beginning, became alarmed.

On 15th February 1898 there was an explosion aboard the *Maine*, a United States battle ship moored in the port of Havana, and the ship was sunk. This was seen as a *casus belli* by Washington and war was declared on Madrid. The conflict did not last long, but it had disastrous results for Spain, which had been caught up in the patriotic fervour of its unwary leaders. The weak Spanish fleet, made up of a small collection of old ships, could do little against the powerful American squadron and suffered a calamitous defeat at Cavite in the Philippines and Santiago in Cuba. Spain had no option but to acquiesce to the Treaty of Paris (1898), which signed Cuba, Puerto Rico and the Philippines over to the United States in return for only a token economic compensation.

News of the defeat caused a wave of commotion in the Spanish capital. It signified the fall of the glorious Hispanoamerican Empire. In all walks of Spanish society the people opened their arms to Europe and their minds to new thinking and values. Its manifestation in politics was known as the Regenerationism movement, and was also expressed in an important period of Spanish literature by the 'Generation of 98', which included some of Spain's most celebrated authors, such as Unamuno, Ramiro de Maeztu, Pío Baroja, Juan Ramón Jiménez, Azorín, and Antonio Machado.

CHAPTER III

MILITARY MAN AND JOURNALIST
IN CUBA AND INDIA

At that time, England was going through a period when it was not waging colonial wars. The Victorian reign ended with a peaceful decade, which military men despaired of, since they could thus not aspire to exercising their profession in an honourable and dignified way.

This being the situation, Churchill and his friend Barnes requested a transfer to Cuba, where the Spanish were facing a dangerous revolt. There they worked as observers along-side the Spanish army. In addition, Churchill had managed to get the *Daily Graphic* to name him their correspondent in Cuba in order to cover the war.

That would be Churchill's first important journey. He had already travelled to France and Switzerland, but he had never gone to another continent.

The first stage of the journey ended in New York, where they spent a few days at the home of friends of Churchill's mother. From New York they went to Cuba, where they were received by the military governor of the island, Martínez Campos. At the two friends' request, they were promptly sent to General Valdés's column, where his troops were making a two-week expedition through the rebel zone in order to relieve the isolated garrisons. The column went from one for-tified post to another, and at times the enemies took them by surprise. One of the fights that they had with the insurgents took place precisely on Churchill's twentieth birthday.

Aside from this, Winston Churchill's stay in Cuba was quite short. The second lieutenant returned to his regiment before the Americans secured the rebels' victory, just when the 4th Hussars were to set sail for India.

For the two thousand two hundred soldiers and officers in the regiment, an almost month-long journey would begin on 11th September 1896, which would leave them in Bombay, on board a troop transport boat christened the *Britannia*.

Once in Bombay, a military train took them to Bangalore, a city in the state of Mysore in the southern part of the Asian continent.

Life in Bangalore

The climate in Bangalore was excellent, since the city is at an altitude of more than three thousand feet. Even so, it was quite hot, although not enough to make life unpleasant.

With his inseparable friends, Barnes and Baring, Churchill rented a splendid flat covered with bougainvillea and roses. They engaged the services of an Indian butler who did everything for them: he tidied the flat and cooked himself. Churchill and his friends only had to turn over to him the payments they received from the army, and the butler took care of everything.

It should be said that the pay they received was minimum. The friends had to ensure that their families sent them more money, because fourteen shillings per day and three pounds to maintain their horses was not even enough to live badly. Winston Churchill received five hundred pounds from his family.

The typical day was quite monotonous: at six in the morning the regiment began its exercises; and from breakfast until

At twenty years of age, showing off his Hussars uniform.

the end of the afternoon they had no scheduled activities. When the sun went down, the soldiers' only distraction was polo, a sport that Churchill came to master like a true champion. The regiment of which Churchill formed part aimed to win the annual cup in Hyderabad.

During his free time, Churchill read books, which led him to devote himself to journalism. Among his favourite authors at that time were names such as Plato, Aristotle, Malthus, Schopenhauer, Darwin, Gibbon, Macaulay and Montgomery, as well as many more. He also spent his time catching butterflies and caring for the rosebushes at his flat.

During a brief stay in London while on leave, Churchill found out through the newspapers about an insurrection in India by Pathan tribesmen, on the north-west frontier. But unfortunately for him, upon his return to Bangalore he was not included in the expedition that went to face those hostile tribes.

He then tried to get transferred. Using his contacts, he finally managed to be accepted as the war correspondent for the Allahabad newspaper *Pioneer*. He asked the 4th Hussars for a month's leave of absence, and he went to the Indian north-west frontier to cover the events there. Inactivity had ended for young Churchill.

He met up with General Bindon Blood at Malakand Field. The general had offered him a post among his troops as war correspondent. He wanted to demonstrate the British power when facing the insurgents. But when the troops reached Mammund, they were heavily attacked and there were more than forty casualties amongst soldiers and officers. Bindon Blood ordered General Jeffreys, who commanded the second brigade, to go down into the valley and attack the tribesmen. Churchill immediately found a place in General Jeffreys's column. After two weeks of furious fighting, the Mammund valley was once again in British hands.

The operations then continued in the north-west against the Afridis, and meanwhile, in both Allahabad and London – he also wrote for the *Daily Telegraph* – the chronicles that came from Winston Churchill's pen were regularly published, signed with the pseudonym 'A young officer'.

Criticism and comments were quite positive, so Winston Churchill then decided to publish his first book: *The Story of the Malakand Field Force*, where he wrote an account of the campaign in which he participated under the orders of General Bindon Blood. This was to be his first book, the first in a long series of Churchill's personal experiences. He even received personal congratulations from the Prince of Wales for this book.

After this first book, Churchill undertook the task of writing a war novel, which he published under the title *Savrola*, but this did not achieve the same recognition as his first chronicle. Nevertheless, the journal that published his writing paid him approximately seven hundred pounds for it, about five times his annual salary as an officer. Winston had taken two months to write *Savrola*. In the plot he mixed love and politics, with the president of an imaginary European country using his wife to put an end to the opposition leader. But, as we have already mentioned, the novel was quite weak and its reception was unfavourable. Several years later, Churchill declared that he always advised his friends not to read this book.

When the campaign on the Indian border ended, Churchill returned to Bangalore. The success of his first book and his war chronicles had been so great that he started to receive proposals from newspaper editors and editors-in-chief. He liked to write, but at twenty-three years old he still preferred the excitement of the battlefield.

Then, the government of Lord Salisbury, at that time Prime Minister of England, decided to wage a campaign against the Sudan.

Churchill took advantage of the opportunity to request another transfer, this time to Egypt, in order to participate in the announced campaign. Although his transfer was denied at first, through the Duke of Marlborough's family connections he finally managed to be sent to the 21st Lancers regiment, which formed part of the Anglo-Egyptian army.

CHAPTER IV

WINSTON CHURCHILL IN EGYPT

The River War

Churchill had to travel to the Sudan by his own means, at his own cost, and in the event of being injured, he would not receive the pension normally due. Nevertheless, he had the payments he earned from the *Morning Post* to work as its correspondent.

At the end of July 1898, Churchill arrived in Cairo. At the beginning of the following month, the 21st Lancers left in a special train for Assiut. From there they headed for Aswan and later for Wadi Halfa. From there they took a train that left them in the Sudan.

Thus began an exciting trip that would take him all along the Nile. This would be the beginning of another book written by Churchill, *The River War*.

In the middle of August, the 21st Lancers reached the camp at Atbara in the Sudan. They then marched on to Khartoum, travelling yet another two hundred miles or so.

Churchill was concerned because he was under the orders of a man that had most obstinately opposed his transfer from India. He might receive orders to return, and this would especially affect the *Morning Post*, which had placed its trust in him as its correspondent.

Khartoum had been built in 1822 at the place where the first Egyptian conqueror, Ismael Pasha, had camped. The city was located on the banks of the Blue Nile, almost at its confluence with the White Nile, near the city of Omdurman, where the Mahdist dervishes who had taken Khartoum in 1885 and assassinated the English general, Gordon, had built forts. Precisely, one of the objectives of the Lancers' expedition was to avenge the death of General Gordon.

The Anglo-Egyptian troops faced the dervish army on 1st September 1898. They were headed by the 21st Lancers. On 2nd September, the Lancers initiated the offensive. With his lieutenant's stripes, Churchill went with the advance patrol of the 4th Lancers. It was not long before the first confrontation between the dervish tribesmen and units of the Anglo-Egyptian army took place. Churchill did not carry a sword, since he did not trust the injury to his right shoulder which he had suffered many years back. Instead he used a Mauser pistol, which he had bought in London and with which he could face enemies who would otherwise have put an end to his life.

That very afternoon, Khartoum and Omdurman returned to British hands, and Gordon had been avenged.

Churchill began to write his articles for the *Morning Post* and gather enough material to write *The River War*.

Shortly after he returned to London. At that time, Churchill thought the moment had come for him to retire from the army. He considered the salary as an official to be very meagre, and he could not be dependent on his family for life for the five hundred pounds he received from them. Thus, he decided to devote 1899 to returning to India in order to win the polo championship with the 4th Hussars, write his book on the Sudan war and other articles in order finally to leave the army, and gain a seat in the English parliament.

CHAPTER V

WINSTON CHURCHILL'S POLITICAL CAREER BEGINS

Winston Churchill returned to England in the middle of 1889. [1899]
He was twenty-five years old at the time.

His relationship with his mother had improved quite a lot since she had been widowed. At that time, she used all her influence to open any door for her son, in whom she had placed all her hopes and trust.

In this way, Churchill, conservative in his political ideas, managed to get Lord Salisbury to present his candidacy for Oldham, Lancashire, since the former MP had recently died. Churchill dedicated himself wholeheartedly to the campaign with the same keenness that characterised him throughout his whole life.

However, when the election results were announced, Churchill had been defeated by his adversary, albeit not by a great margin.

This first campaign made Churchill spend many hours practising his skills as a speaker, since he was not exactly born with a gift for words. But from that moment on, thanks to his amazing willpower, his speeches were always eloquent and moving.

The war in South Africa

At that time, the political situation in England was as follows:

31

The 1885 elections for the House of Commons had brought the Liberals to power. However, in the following year, 1886, they had been defeated by the Conservative party.

While the Liberals were in power, they had fomented a social policy that regulated the working conditions of children and miners; they had also extended public education and had begun to build economical housing for workers. However, during their term of office they did not solve the problems that England still had with Ireland. The Liberals themselves ended up divided because they were not sure how to best deal with the matter.

On the other hand, after gaining a foothold in South Africa on the heels of the Napoleonic Wars, England had attempted to force the Dutch and even French colonists toward the North. And in that wild country the Boers had founded two republics, Orange and the Transvaal, which were in permanent conflict with the English authorities in Cape Town.

With the discovery of the gold mines in the Transvaal, the conflict took on a more violent slant, since the English defended the rights of the miners, who were against the Boers. In 1885 a conflict started as a result of the incursion by Doctor Jameson, who decided to raise a private army in order to annex Orange and the Transvaal for England.

The attempt failed and London condemned Jameson, but the Uitlanders were making themselves heard more and more in Johannesburg, and the English people of Cape Town were giving them more and more assistance. Finally, on 11th October 1889 war broke out when President Kruger called on the British government to withdraw its troops from the borders with the states founded by the Boers. Joseph Chamberlain, at that time the English Minister of War, sent a communiqué to the governor of the British Cape Town colony instructing him to inform Pretoria, the capital of the Transvaal, that the conditions imposed by the government of the Republic were such that the British government considered discussions useless.

The South African war had broken out. However, in the eyes of the English population it was a mere military march.

Churchill, following his tradition, went straight to the *Morning Post* in order to be appointed war correspondent.

Once he reached Cape Town, as a good chronicler of events, he immediately wanted to reach the front line, but he took a train that derailed. He was then made prisoner by Louis Botha, who years would later be the Prime Minister of the South African Union and a personal friend of Winston Churchill.

At that time, however, he was only the enemy. Churchill was escorted to Pretoria, where he was incarcerated in a former elementary school. In fact, it was not a real prison since the walls were not very high and there were few guards. One night, Churchill attempted to escape with two other companions. He was the only one who managed to clamber over the low wall, because his companions, frightened by the sound of the sentinels' footsteps, gave up their attempt.

Then began several days in which he wandered through the enemy territory, hiding in bushes with hardly any provisions to eat.

Luckily, he met up with an Englishman whom the Boers had left to guard a mine in an area far from the battlefield. He hid in a hut and was finally stowed away on a train heading toward Mozambique.

But the Boers offered a reward of twenty-five pounds for anyone who could find, dead or alive, an escaped prisoner of war, Winston Churchill. In the army quarters where the reward was offered there was a description of the escaped man, which serves to give us an idea of how Churchill appeared at that time:

33

Englishman, twenty-five years old; approximate height, 5 ft. 8 in.; medium build; walks leaning slightly forward; pale complexion; dark reddish-coloured hair; small barely-visible moustache; speaks with a nasal accent and cannot pronounce the "s" sound correctly.

When Churchill reached his destination he quickly telegraphed his adventures to the *Morning Post* and immediately requested permission once again to combine the post of war correspondent with that of an officer in an irregular cavalry regiment. On 3rd March 1900 he took part in the liberation of Ladysmith. Pretoria, the capital of the Transvaal, surrendered during the month of May.

Despite the fact that the war appeared to have ended, in fact it had not. But Churchill decided that it was time to go back, and in July 1900 he returned to England.

In South Africa, outside the cities, the Boer forces led by General Botha waged an exhausting guerilla war for two years. General Kitchener, hero of the war with the Mahdi, responded with harsh repression that led to the civil population being detained in concentration camps and a scorched earth policy. Botha finally surrendered at Verrening on 31st May 1902, but the new British colonies, the Transvaal and Orange, with Boer majorities, gained administrative independence. Afrikaans was recognised as an official language, and Great Britain offered aid to reconstruct the country.

The war had cost England 22,000 dead and a deep humiliation in its pride as an imperial power, despite its Pyrrhic victory.

CHAPTER VI

THE RUNGS OF POWER

When the boat that went from South Africa to the British Isles reached its port of call, Churchill was a famous name. He had gained a great deal of publicity thanks to his daring and valour, to the escape he recounted in his chronicles, to his newspaper articles and partly to his novels as well.

At the time the political situation in English pointed toward the dissolution of Parliament, with the consequent elections. Churchill once again ran for Oldham, where the conservatives held him in high esteem.

The elections were held at the end of September, and thanks to a great publicity campaign, Winston Churchill obtained two hundred twenty-two votes more than his opponent, the Liberal Runciman.

Thus Churchill began his parliamentary career, with a Conservative majority of one hundred thirty-four seats. Lord Salisbury continued to head the government.

Churchill's first speech in Parliament was brought about due to a controversy on the war in South Africa. In short, he said that England should do whatever was in its power to put a glorious end to its wartime operations, but that afterwards it ought to treat its enemies generously.

At the same time, Churchill moved to London and adopted the same everyday lifestyle that his father had led. He moved into a flat at 105 Mount Street and for income he earned copyright allowances from his books, as well as his pay as a Member of Parliament.

However, despite his intense social life, Churchill also worked tirelessly. In addition to writing books, he gave talks throughout the country and attended all the sessions at the House of Commons.

Nevertheless, his political dynamism contrasted with the lack of cohesion in the Conservative party. Together with several friends, Churchill then decided to found a small group of MPs who diverged from the Tories to some degree. They called themselves the Hooligans, and they met every Thursday for dinner, accompanied by different political personalities, both Conservative and Liberal.

At that time, Churchill realised that the conservative world was on the decline at the beginning of the 20th century.

That same year, 1902, Lord Salisbury had to give up his post as Prime Minister for health reasons, and he was replaced by Arthur James Balfour, Salisbury's nephew. Yet despite this family relationship, Balfour did not have as much power as his uncle within the party, which was more and more divided, especially with regard to the pressing matters of the time.

During the early months of 1904 the situation within the Conservative party went from bad to worse. Once, during a debate on social unrest, Churchill requested that the rights of the labour unions be clearly defined, in a speech which the press termed as Liberal or even Labour.

The following day, when Churchill entered in the hall of the House of Commons, instead of sitting at his usual seat, he crossed the hall and took a seat next to Lloyd George, in the seat his father had occupied when he was in the opposition. The initiative caused a sensation – it should be remembered that Churchill loved these *coups de théâtre*.

This was an act of bravery which meant not only abandoning his party but also breaking with his accustomed milieu.

With his mother during his time as Lord of the Admiralty, in 1912.

Churchill himself would later write the following about Lloyd George:

> *Naturally, a man like Lloyd George was going to exercise great influence over me. When I crossed the threshold of the House and left the Conservative party in 1904, I took a seat by his side. Ever since then we have worked together, certainly not without differences and even disputes; but on the most important matters we practically worked in constant association for almost twenty years. He was the greatest master I have ever known in the art of making people do things and fully seeing them through to the end; no other British politician has effectively possessed in my days his competence for moving men and enterprises. When the history of the first quarter of this century is written, it will be seen that the greatest part of our fortune, in peace as in war, was shaped by the hands of this man. He gave orthodox Liberalism the new inflection of an ardent social policy. All the great insurance plans have entered into the life of the English people either created or promoted by him. He launched our finances along the path of the progressive taxation on wealth as an equalising factor in social life. In the sombre days of war he took on supreme power and grasped it vigorously until overwhelming victory was achieved. He, for better or worse, resolved the Irish question or at least separated it from the main avenue of the British Empire. All of these matters belong, in fact, to history. Nowadays, strong currents of censure, or at least disapproval, are working against the most important*

*deeds of his life. His merits might be contested, but
nobody can dispute their magnitude.*

His relationship with the Liberals

His new political friends mistrusted Churchill for quite
some time, since they considered his spectacular gesture of
moving over to the opposition as unsporting.

However, Churchill grew with adversity. Since it was
unthinkable for him to run for Oldham, the Liberals began to
search for a new constituency where he could stand. They
chose Manchester, which was quite promising because there
was support for his free-trade ideas, which had more than
anything led him to renounce his conservatism.

The early contacts with the Manchester constituency gave
favourable results. In October 1904, the still MP for Oldham
undertook a series of talks and public meetings in which he
harshly attacked the Balfour government.

At the end of 1905, Balfour presented his resignation. Two
possible solutions were considered: the first involved dis-
solving the House and bringing the elections forward; and
second was based on submitting his resignation to King
Edward VII, who had succeeded Queen Victoria in 1901, and
who would then be forced to call on the head of the Liberal
party.

The latter solution had more advantages than the former,
since in this way the Liberals would continue to have a minority in the House of Commons, and Campbell-Bannermann
would have a hard time forming a government. Balfour thus
chose the latter option.

The Liberal party leader then tried to build his team. From
the start he planned to offer Winston Churchill the post of
Under-Secretary of State in the Exchequer.

39

This offer was quite tempting, but Churchill refused it, preferring to choose the portfolio of the Colonial Office. Anyone else but the future Prime Minister Winston Churchill would have accepted it, but he was very ambitious and did not want to occupy a secondary post under the Chancellor of the Exchequer, the real Finance Minister.

However, since the portfolio of the Colonies pertained to Lord Elgin and he spent most of his time at his Scottish retreat, he would leave his associate a great deal of freedom. Furthermore, Lord Elgin had a seat in the House of Lords, so that Winston Churchill would represent the ministry in the House of Commons debates. This would allow him to continue his political career as he thought best.

Thus he negotiated this possibility, and indeed he got his wish. He had just turned thirty-one years old.

CHAPTER VII

AN ARDUOUS TASK IN THE MINISTRIES

Recently named Under-Secretary of the Ministry of the Colonies, Churchill had to appoint a private secretary. The person he chose was Edward Marsh, a young man from a good family who was thirty-three years old at the time. The choice was a good one, since from that moment on a life-long friendship was to develop between the two men.

However, for the time being what interested the new Prime Minister of England was to get general elections called as soon as possible, since he wanted to take advantage of the Liberal upswing and especially the crisis in the Conservative party.

Edward VII dissolved Parliament at the beginning of 1906 and set the date of 13th February for its re-opening. However, since this had been known in advance, the election campaigns had begun days earlier. Thus, Churchill had been devoting himself to Manchester since 4th January.

The campaign was quite lively all over England. In Manchester, voting took place on 13th January. Churchill won the elections in this city by an overwhelming majority.

Once back in London, he practically ran the portfolio of the Ministry of the Colonies alone, since Lord Elgin was spending more and more time in Scotland. He also had time left to write, since shortly after winning the elections the Macmillan publishing house brought out Lord Randolph's biography, whose author was none other than Winston Churchill. The critics were quite favourable, and some people even said that Winston Churchilll figured among the literary elite.

With regard to his work in the Ministry of the Colonies, one of the Under-Secretary's main concerns was organising the situation in South Africa. The Boers, who could no longer fight on the battlefield, now did so on the political front. Churchill was sure that the solution to the conflict could only be reached through total reconciliation with the Boers, and he worked tirelessly to achieve this. Obviously he was not facing either the blacks or the Indians but the Dutch, and this led him to sign a statute that would involve broad autonomy, similar to that of Canada. After the proclaimed Constitution granted by Edward VII, on 20th February 1907 elections were held in the Transvaal. The Het Volt Boer party won a majority, and Louis Botha was named Prime Minister.

In addition to his work in the Ministry of the Colonies, Churchill attended to other government matters. In 1906, at the Kaiser's invitation, he attended the Imperial Army's manoeuvres in Breslau. In 1907 as well he was present at the great French manoeuvres and travelled through East Africa.

Based on his observations and conclusions, he presented Lord Elgin and the Ministry of War with an extensive report on the arming of the English forces overseas. He even published, as was his wont, several articles in *Strand Magazine* and had time to write a book entitled *My Africa Journey*, which once again was well received among literary enthusiasts.

The Ministry of Trade

In 1908 Prime Minister Campbell-Bannermann resigned, as he was seriously ill, and he was succeeded by Herbert Henry Asquith.

Asquith formed a new government and thought that Winston Churchill could occupy a post as a Minister. There were three possibilities: the Colonies, the Admiralty or Public Assistance. Naturally, Churchill would have preferred the Ministry of the Colonies, since he had complete mastery of the matter; however, the portfolio assigned to him in the end was none of the above. He was given the Ministry of Trade.

In democratic England, a Minister named by succession had to face an election to ratify his office. And then an extraordinary event took place: Churchill was defeated in Manchester by his Conservative rival. The difference in votes was tiny, but enough for him not to be elected. This took place precisely because Churchill had ignored his constituency to focus on his work in the Ministry of the Colonies, a fact that had been seized on by the Conservatives, who had done their utmost to defeat him.

However, the Liberals then had him run for Dundee, where the post had been left vacant. In the pre-election campaign, Churchill especially emphasised the social aspects of the city and broadly expounded on his liberal theses in favour of the workers. All of this helped him to defeat even the candidate presented by the Labour Party, who was more leftist than the Liberal.

Herbert Henry Asquith had been born in Morley, Yorkshire in 1852. He was extraordinarily cultured and his letters were filled with literary quotations. He was a man of great personal charm, quick to make decisions, with a calm and balanced personality. His career as a jurist took off early. In 1866 he won a seat in the House of Commons for the Liberal party. He then took on the portfolios of Interior and the Exchequer in 1905, and three years later, Edward VII asked him to form a government.

A 1908 plan granted British people over the age of seventy who had a weekly income of not more than ten shillings a pension of five shillings per week. The Asquith government also focused on a general insurance against illness and unemployment; but where would he get the funds he needed? The response came quickly in the Welsh-accented English of David Lloyd George, forty-five years of age and Minister of the Exchequer.

The years before World War I were as tumultuous in Great Britain as in other countries. There had not been such a violent atmosphere in the House of Commons for some time. Two personalities especially raised emotions: David Lloyd George, Chancellor of the Treasury, democratic, radical, pacifist and a singer of psalms; and Winston Churchill. Both were totally different, although this did not stop them from being close friends; together they would vigorously attack the wealthy, the Conservatives, the aristocrats and the old structures they wanted to reform.

Lloyd George was born in a small town in Wales to a humble family, and he never forgot the deprivations of his youth. His education was limited to that of a rural school, but young David would not cease to prosper despite this. In 1890 he entered the House of Commons, elected by Welsh nationalists, and he showed himself to be dynamic, eloquent, passionate and even unscrupulous. In the middle of the Boer War, he attacked imperialism and its promoters. He was Minister of Trade in 1905 and excelled in his modern organisation of the Port of London. But the measure of his peak performance would come in 1908, and later in the Exchequer, the key post and touchstone of great statesmen and the second most powerful position in the government. He had already presented a plan: devote to the fight against poverty money that he would not squander on the army and the navy, two instruments of imperialism and reactionary thinking, in his view. The rich would pay for his reforms, he announced baldly to his colleagues.

CHAPTER VIII

WINSTON CHURCHILL GETS MARRIED

Churchill's wedding with Clementine

Churchill had spent the previous Sunday, 12th April, with his mother at Salisbury Hall. He had just been named Minister of Trade but had not yet run for re-election in Manchester.

That day he met the girl that would later become his wife, Clementine Hozier, a pretty young Scottish girl, not wealthy, although from a good family, and the niece of the Count of Airlie.

Clementine had been born on 1st April 1885. She had finished her studies, part of which she had taken at the Sorbonne, and she spoke flawless French and German.

During the period following their meeting on 12th April, since Churchill had to attend to his election in Manchester and then in Dundee, his relations with the young woman were virtually reduced to written correspondence. But the letters showed ever greater closeness between the two. Finally, the matter of his being appointed Minister of the Interior for Trade having been resolved, Clementine was invited to spend a few days in the Duke of Marlborough's castle, where she arrived on 10th August.

The following day, in the chapel at Blenheim, Winston Churchill asked Clementine to marry him, and she accepted.

The wedding was announced in the *Times* on 15th August, with the news that it was to be held on 12th September that year at two p.m. Everything was so rushed that many personalities who had been invited could not attend since they had to meet other prior engagements.

Winston was thirty-four years old at the time, and Clementine was twenty-three.

After the ceremony, the new couple accompanied their guests to Portland Place, where Lady Helier provided the reception. They spent the first two days of their honeymoon in Blenheim and then went off to Italy to visit Lake Maggiore, ending their honeymoon trip in Venice.

They moved into a flat at 33 Eccleston Square. During their first year of marriage, Clementine announced to Winston that they were going to have a child, and on 11th July 1909 a girl was born, whom they baptised Diana.

Four children would subsequently be born: Randolph, Sarah, Mary and Marigold, although the last would die in 1921, when she was only three years old.

Meanwhile, Churchill skilfully exercised his duties as Minister of Trade. The position also made him the President of the Board of Trade, and the Trade portfolio also included those of Industry and Labour. Winston Churchill was not very familiar with the working class, although he was concerned about them. During his ministry, employment offices came into being, and he fought to establish social security for the unemployed, also getting some laws passed that favoured equal salaries and the institution of a retirement pension after the age of seventy.

During his time as Minister of Trade, Churchill's positions became noticeably closer to those of Lloyd George – who was even one of the witnesses at his wedding – a radicalised liberal who was Chancellor of the Exchequer from 1908 to 1915 and who promoted a review of the power of the Lords and the large monopolies.

Encounter with the Prince of Wales in 1919 in front of the House of Commons.

The House of Lords was made up of aristocrats and nobles, especially of great British landholders, who were staunchly conservative.

Churchill supported Lloyd George in this conflict, since he was sure that the glory of England would depend on the evolution of its people and that in order to triumph it had to remain at the forefront of the most progressive nations.

In the budget that Lloyd George presented for the year 1909, there was a need to increase taxes in order to take better care of the working class in general; these taxes would logically fall on the wealthiest.

At that time an inevitable crisis seemed to be about to break between the two Houses, the House of Commons on the one hand and the Upper Hours or House of Lords, on the other, since the latter had no right to amend the budget, although it conserved the right to reject en bloc.

The crisis took place on 30th November 1909, when the House of Lords rejected Lloyd George's budget by three hundred forty-nine votes to one hundred and four votes.

Elections would be held once again, so on 10th December 1909 the electoral campaigns once again got underway.

Churchill was re-elected by Dundee, but in general the Liberal party did not fare too well. It lost one hundred and four seats, while the Conservatives increased their power considerably.

The Liberals still had a small majority; however, in order to govern, they had to make an alliance with the pro-Labour sector, since the Conservatives only had two seats fewer than the Liberals.

With the re-organisation of the new cabinet, Churchill then took possession of the portfolio of the Interior. He had been offered the position as Minister for Ireland, which he would have liked to accept in memory of his grandfather, the Duke

Viceroy of Dublin, but in the end he went for the more complicated post.

The Labour party's roots went back to 1869, when the British labour unions made efforts to gain working class MPs who were chosen by the Liberal party. This subjection to a non-labour party led the Scottish labour union activist J. Keir Hardie to attempt to organise independent representation. In 1893 he founded the Independent Labour Party, and he undertook the task of getting the majority of labour unions to join it. In their 1899 congress, the unions approved the formula, and in 1900 the Labour Representation Committee was created, which in 1906 adopted the name of Labour party. It was a broad federation of socialist groups and labour unions without its own doctrine; its brief flirtation with the Marxist Social Democratic Federation barely affected its moderate evolutionism. Its growing influence came from its position as referee between the two traditional parties.

The first noble Churchill was General John Churchill, Duke of Marlborough, who was born in the middle of the 17th century in Devonshire. He was educated at the Stuart court; his early successes were due in great measure to James II, and he became one of the great generals. When he realised that James II was blinded by Catholicism, he joined with William of Orange during the Glorious Revolution, and in 1690 he performed major services for the new King William III in Ireland. His imprudent wife, Sarah Jennings, gained him the enmity of the king and queen, and he fell into disgrace, but was rehabilitated in 1698.

He would take on his greatest role during the reign of Queen Ann in the Spanish War of Succession. Marlborough was the supreme commander of the Quadruple Alliance against France. His victories in the Spanish Netherlands were brilliant.

However, poorly supported by the Whig party and attacked by the Tories, he permanently lost the trust of the Queen in

51

1710. With all his duties taken from him, he went into exile on the continent and even contacted James II's former supporters. The arrival of the Hanover dynasty to the English throne led him to regain his titles, but his political role was something of the past. His memory has remained in Spain in a popular song: "*Mambrú se fue a la guerra*".

CHAPTER IX

THE HOME MINISTRY OR MINISTRY OF THE INTERIOR

Churchill's new duties made him change his role as public defender to that of repressor. In effect, the social conflicts England was suffering from during the first decade of the century would lead to a series of general strikes in 1911 that ended up in revolts. During the month of January, a group of anarchists provoked an insurrection on Sidney Street, where the public forces had to intervene in order to oust the demonstrators, who had closed themselves up in an old house.

On 17th December 1910, all of England was frightened and absolutely astounded by reports of an extraordinary crime that filled the newspapers. At ten thirty the previous night, a certain Mr Isenstein, owner of a shop selling fantasy items in Houndsditch, was alarmed by mysterious blows that were coming from the rear of his house. This man called the police. Six officers appeared. Two went to the back of the house, while the sergeant, followed by the other three, went up to the door of the flat where the blows seemed to be coming from. Following the custom that had been common in England until then, the police were unarmed.

The door was half-opened by a man who was asked if he had been working there. Since he did not answer, they continued to ask if there was someone in the house who understood English.

The man left the door ajar and without answering the question, disappeared upstairs. The sergeant pushed the door open and went into a place lit by gaslight. He wished to perform a routine police inquiry, and there did not appear to be any special reason for taking precautions. When they had been there for about one minute, suddenly a door crashed open, a shot rang out and the sergeant toppled to the ground at the doorway. Another shot, this time coming from the staircase, hit the policeman who was advancing from the door; from this door, a man's hand armed with a long pistol slid out; a series of shots were fired and in a few seconds the four officers were dead, dying or wounded in the street. A figure emerged from the house, firing left and right. Only police officer Choate remained, unarmed and injured. Without hesitating, this civil servant rushed at the assassin K despite receiving two new wounds in the chest, and continued to pin him down until he was again injured in the back by another of the criminals and fell dying, riddled by twelve bullets. The gang of assassins, avoiding pursuit by the sixth policeman, who had remained in the rear of the house, disappeared into the darkness and London traffic without leaving any clues for the time being.

Subsequent police investigations showed that a systematic assault and theft operation had been planned not against Mr Isenstein's house, but against that of a woman neighbour who was a jeweller, where merchandise valued at thirty thousand pounds was kept in a safe. The brick wall between the two buildings had been almost totally pierced, and the thieves' tools were found in the tunnel.

At three o'clock the following morning, two women went in search of a doctor in order to attend to a young man who said his name was George Gardstein. He explained that he had been involuntarily injured by a friend with a revolver shot in the back three hours earlier. That man, whose true surname was Morountzef, was the criminal who had killed the police sergeant, and it seems that in the fight with officer Choate one of the bullets that passed through his body had perforated his stomach and lungs. He died before sunrise, leaving a pistol, a dagger and a violin as souvenirs.

We were thus confronted with a type of crime and criminals that England had not seen for generations. Everything pointed to the characteristics of Russian anarchism. It was confirmed that the murderers belonged to a small colony of twenty Latvians from Baltic Russia who, under the guidance of an anarchist known as "Peter the Painter" had looked for a hideout in the heart of London. It was truly the language of those times, a core cell of murder, anarchy and revolution. Those men devoted themselves to carrying out their depraved plots and their dark conspiracies. Although they robbed and murdered for personal ends, their actions were also political in nature. "Peter the Painter" was one of those ferocious beasts who years later, amidst the convulsions of the Great War, was to devour and destroy the Russian state and people.

Scotland Yard used all available means to pursue the criminals. At that time I was Minister of the Interior, and as such I ordered the police to be provided with the best makes of automatic pistol that money could buy. The brave agents that had fallen in the performance of their duty had official burials, and their coffins were draped with the national flag.

In the morning of 3rd January, a telephone called told me:

"The anarchists who murdered the policemen are surrounded at 100 Sidney Street in the East End, from where they are firing against the police using automatic pistols. They have killed a man and they seem to have plenty of ammunition."

I immediately gave the order for the police to use as much force as needed. And I myself went to the scene of the crime.

When I arrived, plans were being made to assault the building simultaneously from various positions. One group, leaving from the door of the building next door, was going to launch itself against the door of the besieged building and go upstairs. Another group of policemen would go in through the back part of the second floor, jumping through a window. A third section, piercing the roof, would jump on the criminals from above. There could be no doubt as to the success of this attack, but the police would surely lose lives, not only from the anarchists' fire, but also by the shots fired in the confusion by the police themselves. Meanwhile, however, the problem solved itself. At approximately one-thirty, a plume of smoke emerged from one of the broken windows in the upper part of the building, and a few minutes later the house was on fire. As the wood crackled and creaked, the *flames roared. Even so, the anarchists, defending themselves from floor to floor, went on firing and the bullets continued to spatter against the walls of the houses and the roadway.*

When the flames started to creep into the lower part of the house, several minutes went by without a single shot being fired by the anarchists.

Finally, at three p.m., the firemen put out the fire. Among the ruins of the building two charred bodies were found, one of them with signs of being struck by an English bullet and the other with traces of being asphyxiated by the smoke.

Thus the Sidney Street battle ended. "Peter the Painter" was never heard of again. He disappeared completely.

The party disputes were then reaching their peak in England, and I was avidly censured in the newspapers and Parliament for my participation in this episode. Mr Balfour, in the House of Commons, was especially sarcastic: "We have seen with interest the photographs that the illustrated newspapers are publishing of the Home Minister at the danger zone. I can understand why the photographer was there; but why was the Minister there?

In another revolt led by the miners in Rhonda, Wales, the police also had to act harshly. As a result, several times Churchill had to confront the Labour party, which had widely criticised him.

Another problem facing Churchill during the time he occupied the position of Home Minister was women's suffrage. In theory, Churchill was not against women voting, since he did not view this discrimination as logical, but he wanted to

57

convince himself that the suffragists' entry onto the political scene would not severely harm the balance of the parties.

As Home Minister, Churchill was under constant surveillance, and he was considered responsible for all the evils that plagued the civil population. However, he did not waver, and he presented all the reports on his actions to the House, the Prime Minister and if need be, to the King himself.

The term 'suffragists' was used in the 19th and early 20th century to denote women who wanted their gender to have the right to vote, before the electoral law had been amended.

The Chartist Movement had supported women's suffrage since 1838; this was also demanded by Cobden and the great Prime Minister Benjamin Disraeli. But the fight for female suffrage dates from the arrival of Stuart Mill to Parliament in 1865, and it had special importance in Great Britain. Due to its impetus, numerous suffragist societies were formed. In 1903, Emmeline Goulden Pankhurst, along with her daughters Christabel and Sylvia, founded the Women's Social and Political Union, which waged a campaign in favour of the vote for women. The movement also had a militant side; meetings became more frequent and opposition to Prime Minister Asquith led to violent demonstrations and numerous arrests. In 1917, the suffragists would gain partial voting rights, since the vote was granted to women over the age of 30 who headed a family, and in 1928 women were granted the right to vote without restrictions.

The situation in Ireland was explosive. At the end of the 19th century the island's population had drastically decreased because of the "great famine" brought about by the poor potato harvest, especially during the period 1846-1848. More than two million Irish people had emigrated to the US, among them the ancestors of the Kennedy clan. The reforms undertaken by Gladstone's liberal government could not contain the Irish, who as of 1870 began to demand autonomy, which they called home rule, but the plan failed in the British Parliament in 1886 and 1893.

The nationalists, grouped into secret societies such as Sinn Fein ('We Alone'), did not hesitate to use violence against the British and the Protestant minority who, tightly massed in Ulster, were opposed to any anything that would separate them from the London government. The outbreak of World War I led to a postponement of home rule, which had been set for 1914. The 1916 Easter Rebellion would be brutally crushed, although the rebels' sacrifices were protested by the other free nations. After the formation of two parliaments, one in Belfast and another in Dublin, and the triumph of Sinn Fein in the Dublin elections, a true civil war broke out (1919-1921). The new Irish Free State was born in 1921, with its capital in Dublin, while the northern part of the island remained part of Great Britain.

CHAPTER X

FIRST LORD OF THE ADMIRALTY

During the second half of 1911, a great concern bristled in England: the crisis between Germany and France over Morocco could lead to war, and if it got involved in a war, England would be compromised by a treaty it had signed with France in 1904, the *Entente Cordiale*, through which they put an end to their confrontations over colonial issues and instituted a policy of unity in international matters.

From that moment on, the English did their best to organise a well-armed navy based on new structures.

Asquith suddenly asked Churchill to change portfolios from the Home Office to the Navy, based on a series of reports that he had made on the lack of co-ordination between the Army and the Navy. We should never forget that even though Churchill only held one office in the Government, he liked to know about everything and if he could, he liked to get involved in all matters. Thus, who better than Winston Churchill to occupy the post of First Lord of the Admiralty?

Churchill accepted the offer almost without hesitation; and in October 1911 he was appointed First Lord of the Admiralty.

This appointment was not well received among Naval professionals. During the time when he had been a liberal MP, Churchill had always defined himself as a pacifist, and he had even disapproved of the Navy's budgets, claiming that social issues deserved more attention than war matters.

However, in order to put a stop to the rumours and avoid being viewed as incompetent, he chose as his personal adviser Lord Fisher, a former Sea Lord who had just retired, with whom he got along well.

During his term of office, Lord Fisher had modernised the English Navy in many ways: it had been his idea to build the Dreadnoughts, the modern English fighting ships. He had also undertaken reforms in the field of instruction and the recruiting system, and he fomented the construction of submarines.

Upon his appointment, Churchill immediately announced that he was planning a series of innovations, among them the need to create a General Navy Staff, who could liase with their Army counterpart.

Of course at that time Churchill could not have known that he had so little time to prepare the Navy for a war.

But it did not take long for him to win the sympathies of the sailors, albeit at the expense of good relations with the Government since, in order to subsidise the innovations he had in mind, his budget was exorbitant. His programme for enlarging the Naval fleet involved building two Dreadnoughts for every one built by the Germany Navy and, above all, enlarging the submarine fleet.

Nevertheless, Churchill managed to get the budget he presented passed. It must be recalled that this was in the middle of the age of 'armed peace', when almost all nations in Europe feared a future war and applied the ancient Roman concept of *si vis pax, para bellum*, that is, if you want peace, prepare for war.

In reality, the arms race worried the entire British government so much that, as the result of an initiative by the Kaiser, the English Minister of War went to Berlin in order to forge an agreement before war broke out. But this was not to be: the Germans agreed to slow down their ship building pro-

Opening speech in Parliament in December 1921.

63

gramme only in exchange for England's neutrality in case of conflict. Logically, this would have meant severing the *Entente Cordiale*, and conversations were broken off.

Winston Churchill was pleased that no agreement was reached, and from that moment on not only did he devote himself to the naval fleet, but he also fully immersed himself in the field of aviation, since he had the brilliant idea that both corps should be closely united in order to support and reinforce one another mutually. He had understood the role that aviation should play in the rapidly approaching conflict.

The appearance of the battleship Dreadnought, (which means "fear nothing") transformed navies all over the world. The enormous, sensational features of this new vessel left all the others completely antiquated, leading other countries to attempt to copy the British by building their own 'Dreadnoughts', a name used to refer to battleships for many years.

They did not hold intermediate artillery as in old times. Its ten 305 mm single-calibre guns provided a broadside of more than 3 tonnes, with the longest range known until then. This fire power and range imposed long-distance combat, preventing any other force from approaching without considerable risk.

Its propulsion system provided a higher speed, reaching up to 21.6 knots. Since in its time it was inaccessible to the fire of other units, the proper but risky decision was taken to provide it with little armour in favour of speed. It displaced about 22,000 tonnes at full load, and it was 525 ft long.

With regard to the air, in 1910 the American brothers Wilbur and Orville Wright had managed to build an apparatus heavier than air which could remain airborne for a few seconds at a certain height. From then on, it was constantly being perfected. The European nations, with England at the fore, began to build them.

This new invention, at first used for observation, would soon compete favourably against the antiquated zeppelin or dirigible, which had been designed by the German Count Zeppelin (1838-1917).

Churchill also modernised the submarine fleet. The underwater ship had been a Spanish invention by Narciso Monturiol (1859) and Isaac Peral (1880), which was used in war when provided with torpedoes, its most effective means of attack.

On the eve of the great conflict, Churchill instructed the naval engineers to study the possibility of building an armoured vehicle that could pass over trenches. Thus the combat tank emerged, conceived as a war vehicle which was heavily protected and armoured, and which by moving over a flexible wheel or rotating chain, it could cross the roughest terrain.

By using the tank, the British were attempting to resuscitate the old Roman 'testudo' or turtle. The secrecy under which the new vehicles were developed, which led people to believe while they were being built that they were actually enormous water tanks for the Army's drinking purposes, made this anecdotal name spread.

Thus the tank was born, and its earliest small-sized model was called Little Willie. The eighteen tanks built were quite properly called "Winston's folly".

CHAPTER XI

WORLD WAR I BREAKS OUT

A few months later, in 1914, the conflict broke out.

The detonator was the assassination of Archduke Francis Ferdinand in Sarajevo by a Serbian nationalist on 28 June. Austria-Hungary declared war against Serbia and Europe thus entered an irreversible process.

During the entire month of July, Europe desperately sought a reconciliation, but on 3rd August the German troops entered Belgium and France. Great Britain, for its part, sent an ultimatum to Germany which was ignored, and on 4th August it was announced from the Admiralty that hostilities against Germany were beginning.

The English fleet was ready. England had twenty-two Dreadnoughts and another twelve in the dockyards, while the German fleet only had sixteen completed and another four under construction.

The English fleet was also able to protect the expeditionary corps that crossed the English Channel on 8th and 22nd August to disembark at Dunkirk, Bologne and Le Havre.

However, the war started to last longer than predicted, and at the end of August it stabilised on the seas, where a lengthy conflict had already been predicted.

At that time, Churchill came up with two plans: first, the occupation of the island of Borkum in the Baltic Sea, and second, the conquest of the Dardanelles and the consequent capitulation of Constantinople, which would lead to the fall of the

Ottoman Empire and allow the allies to help the Russians, who were being left without resources, in order to unleash a massive attack against the Germans.

Lord Fisher was against the latter operation. Churchill also preferred the former, but when the Cabinet voted in favour of the Dardanelles, he went over to the majority.

The Dardanelles operation fails

Thus, on 19th February 1915, the English naval fleet prepared to attack the Dardanelles. It had to be a quick operation since surprise attacks were the Anglo-French fleet's best ally. But there were setbacks due to both bad weather and the time needed to dredge the canal.

This situation was taken advantage of by the Turks by reinforcing their garrisons and artillery.

On 18th March the fleet was ready to attack at the Strait of Cannakale, but two English and one French vessel were sunk as a result of running into unlocated mines.

The development of events was being followed in London not without despair. Asquith's cabinet then, against Churchill's wishes, decided that there would have to be a landing. On 25th April, the troops disembarked at Gallipoli, but they were blocked on the beach itself. The Dardanelles operation concluded in total failure at the end of 1915.

A scapegoat had to be found in London, and this was none other than Winston Churchill. Fisher resigned in May as First Sea Lord after making public his differences with the First Lord of the Admiralty. The Conservatives seized the occasion to ask that their party be allowed to participate in the government. This was accepted, and thus on 26th May the British government was made up of twelve Liberal ministers, eight Conservatives and one Labour. Winston Churchill was replaced in his portfolio by Balfour. He was almost convinced that his political career was over then.

Winston Churchill in the trenches

Churchill left for the country with Clementine and their children. For a short time he devoted himself to painting – his love of painting emerged during this period – but in the end he decided to go to the front.

He gave up his seat as Member of Parliament for Dundee in November in order to join a battalion of Grenadier Guards. Shortly after, he was sent to the 6th Royal Scots Fusiliers with the rank of Lieutenant Colonel.

But Churchill was not happy. His battalion did not take part in any major operations. This is how he spent 1916. The war was going badly for England because the zeppelins were increasing their incursions into its territory and many ships of war and especially men were being lost.

Churchill could not bear it any longer and requested to return to his seat as MP in the House of Commons. The High Command, which had never looked kindly upon his presence at the front, heartily agreed.

The year 1917 was disastrous on all fronts. But in April the United States declared war against the Germans as a result of the sinking of the *Lusitania*.

Once again occupying his seat in the House of Commons, Churchill presented his conclusions as to why the United States had joined the allied front. His speech, in which he advocated suspending bloody actions until the Americans' arrival, was listened to by everyone and approved. In addition, it coincided with the publication of the report on the expedition against the Dardanelles, in which Churchill came out well.

This report was enough for Lloyd George, at that time Primer Minister since Asquith's death, appointed Churchill as Minister for Armament and Munitions.

Winston plunged into his new job. This ministry was an enormous bureaucratic machine which he managed to streamline and rationalise and whose productivity he even managed to increase.

He worked more than fifteen hours a day, planning the production of war material and the construction of new weapons, such as tanks with caterpillar wheels. Indeed, English tanks appeared for the first time in the English army in November 1917.

The year 1918 marked the end of the war. The German disaster began to take shape in August 1918, and on 11th November of that same year, the Germans signed the armistice in the Compiègne woods outside Paris, in a railway car. The long conflict had caused terrible demographic losses. There were more than ten million dead. Germany lost 1,800,000 men, twelve percent of its men between the ages of 15 and 50; France lost 1,400,000; the United Kingdom lost almost 750,000; Russia almost 3 million, to which we must add those who died in the subsequent civil war, which would probably double this number.

In addition to these losses, which had intense demographic repercussions since they especially affected young people and led to a subsequent female over-population, we must add the several million men injured and disabled.

Many families were left fatherless; the vast number of orphans was a concern for the governments.

The material destruction was no less intense; in this aspect, France was the country that was most severely affected. Three million hectares were devastated, the railway network was interrupted, the ports and thousands of buildings destroyed. France's cost for the war was 30% of its national wealth; for

Germany it was 22%, for England 32%, for Italy 26%, and for the United States 9%.

There were wide-ranging social changes as well. The incorporation of women into the workforce, until then a male province, increased; the rural exodus toward the cities was quicker; alongside millions of impoverished families there appeared the nouveaux riches, arms manufacturers or speculators, who amassed fortunes. The human archetype of the former soldier, nostalgic for danger, incapable of reintegrating himself into daily life, was the basis of extreme nationalist and revanchist movements.

CHAPTER XII

THE HARSH POST-WAR YEARS

In addition to its innumerable victims, the war noticeably shook the British economy. Between the years 1914 and 1918, exports had practically ceased, while the volume of imports had doubled.

London lost economic power only to concede its position to the country that was becoming the greatest of the great: the United States. The pound sterling lost one-third of its value, while the dollar considerably increased its value on the international market thanks to the loans that America provided to all the needy countries, England, in fact, being one of them.

But England did not only have economic problems. There were also repercussions in the colonies. India was gradually industrialising, to such an extent that it no longer had to depend on England so much. In 1917 the English dominions were recognised as autonomous nations within the Commonwealth.

Lloyd George, taking advantage of the enthusiasm brought about by the armistice, thought general elections should be held in order to approve his appointment of Prime Minister, which had not taken place due to the war.

The results favoured the current prime minister, who after the elections reformed the government, which was a coalition.

Churchill was given the Ministry of War. He mainly had to concern himself with demobilisation. The plan he initially laid out was that the first ones to return home would be the men who occupied specialised positions in industry. But this plan had its detractors, since many of those men had been called to the ranks toward the end of the conflict, and the veterans loudly protested. There were revolts in Calais, Folkestone and Glasgow.

Churchill did not hesitate one moment: he immediately revoked his plan and decided to scale leaves according to length of service. The mutinies then ceased without further ado.

Nor could he set aside national and international matters. From the beginning, Churchill was against the Bolshevik revolution and believed that Great Britain had to help the 'white' forces defeat the 'reds'.

His initiative led to yet another failure. As Minister of War he organised massive arms, munitions and food expeditions for the Russians. But this went against British public opinion. And the most palpable result of this was that later, in 1921, Churchill was forced to leave the Ministry of War in order to once again take up the portfolio of the Colonies.

Trip to Cairo

When he took office as Minister of War, Churchill travelled to Cairo, since the Middle East was in the midst of agitation. The peace conference had created two spheres of influence, the French, which extended over the territory of Syria, and the English, which covered the territory of Palestine. Lawrence of Arabia aspired to having a vast personal dominion with the complicity of the English.

Churchill met personally with Lawrence of Arabia, and together they prepared a plan that Lloyd George's government approved: the idea was to establish a kingdom ruled by Faisal in Iraq and another in Transjordan that would be governed by Faisal's brother, Abdullah.

The problem with Ireland

Once his mission in Cairo ended successfully, Churchill had to face an even greater problem: Ireland.

In 1919, the followers of Sinn Fein had proclaimed the Republic of Ireland and elected as president an Irishman of American origin, Eamon de Valera.

Ireland was practically in a state of urban warfare.

In 1921, King George V himself, successor to Edward VII, went to Belfast to give a speech in a conciliatory tone. Shortly after, Lloyd George asked General Smuts to begin conversations with the leaders of Sinn Fein to get them to agree to meet with an English delegation, of which Winston Churchill logically had to be a member.

Against de Valera's wishes, the Irish agreed and as a result of the conference an agreement was reached that was signed on 11th December 1921, under which Ireland became a Free State with dominion status. But the six counties of Ulster were separated from Irish territory and remained under the Crown.

When the negotiators returned to Dublin, Eamon de Valera de-authorised the treaty and thus a second civil war broke out Ireland, perhaps even more cruel than the previous one, if possible, but one in which the English only took part as spectators. However, in total secrecy, Churchill sent weapons and material in order to support the Free State.

The conflict in Turkey

Yet Winston Churchill's problems did not end there.

In Turkey, the Pasha Mustafa Kemal rebelled and instituted a revolutionary government. After stopping the advance of the Greek army supported by the English, Kemal, at the

75

head of his followers, threatened the city of Cianak, which was defended by English, French and Italians. A few days later, the governments of France and Italy ordered their troops to withdraw to the European coasts. Thus, the English remained alone facing Kemal's warriors.

A new armed conflict could have easily arisen. The British Foreign Minister was in favour of reaching an agreement with Kemal. But with Lloyd George's approval, Churchill, always excited facing the prospect of battle, sent a press release that constituted a true declaration of war, in which it was announced that the British government had decided to reinforce its occupation force in Constantinople and had given the order to oppose the advance of Kemal's troops.

With this declaration they achieved their objective. Kemal withdrew from the siege of Cianak and soon asked for an armistice. The conflict had been resolved.

Churchill here showed his acute vision as a statesman, since shortly afterwards, Kemal deposed the last Sultan, Mehmet VI and proclaimed a new republic of Turkey of which he was elected president in 1923, abolishing the caliphate the next year. In exchange for giving up his claims over bordering territories, in a limited geographical framework he created a western-type Turkish nation, whose capital was moved for symbolic reasons from Istanbul to Ankara, the geographical centre of the new state. The ethnic minorities were reduced, and the Greek minority was exchanged for Turks from European lands. The country was made totally lay: a non-denominational state with the elimination of the Koranic schools, religious tribunals and dervishes. He adopted western civil law, emancipated women, imposed the use of the Gregorian calendar and the use of western weights and measures, and made the Turks westernise their way of dressing (replacing the fez with the hat). He adopted

Churchill's popularity reflected on the streets of London.

the Latin alphabet and made people use their father's last name, which for Kemal was Atatürk, "father of the Turks". With these prospects, it was better to have Turkey as an ally than an enemy.

CHAPTER XIII
NEW ELECTIONS

The conflict in Turkey was over, but English public opinion was indignant and viewed Churchill as a war fanatic.

In addition, at that time, because of the war industries, machinery for production lines had developed considerably. Productivity had moved forward, but due to the appearance of new energy sources, the demand for coal was meagre and miners were left jobless. It was also difficult to export mining production, since the markets were controlled by the United States.

All of this led to several Conservative ministers asking for the dissolution of the governing coalition, and Lloyd George ended up presenting his resignation to the King.

The government that rose to power after Lloyd George's resignation was exclusively made up of Conservatives. Thus, Churchill was unable to be part of it.

However, as was mentioned before, any new government in England must be approved by the voters.

Churchill once again ran for Dundee, but this time things had got complicated. First of all, the working class in his constituency was against someone who wanted to declare war against the Soviets; they also accused him of not having heeded their complaints and especially of being too fond of war.

Furthermore, precisely during the days of the electoral campaign, he suffered an acute attack of appendicitis which required surgery, so that he was only able to participate in one meeting. However, he did send letters to his constituents with the platform he was presenting, and still convalescing, he gave a speech two days before the vote. But it was very poorly received by the persons attending, and his voice could barely be heard above the whistles and the singing of the Communist hymn *The Red Flag* by the reactionaries.

When he was sixty years old, Winston Churchill recalled that campaign with these words:

> *If anyone wants to know anything about elections, let him ask me. I have fought in more parliamentary elections than any of the current members of the House of Commons. I have fought in fifteen of them. Think what that means! Fifteen elections, having to spend at least three weeks on each one, plus the week before and at least one after the elections are held.*
>
> *In 1922, when Lloyd George's governing coalition was dissolved, the force of the new electorate was intact. Precisely three days before the elections I had an attack of appendicitis. Almost too late, I had to undergo a serious operation, and the consequent abdominal wound was seven inches long. My wife and a few friends had to do what they could to sustain the battle as best they could.*
>
> *The tides of time were flowing quickly against us. The meetings everywhere were interrupted and turbulent, not through the efforts of isolated individuals but through general discontent and ill will. Only three days before polling I was allowed to travel to London to the scene. Twenty-five days after my operation, I addressed two large assemblies. The first one was orderly, and I was able to express everything that I had to say. The meeting at night, held at the Drill*

Hall, was a seething mass of eight or nine thousand people, the majority against me. Just remaining on my feet was a hard job, since my wound was still fresh. I had to be transported in a handicapped car to the rostrum and everywhere else. There is no doubt that a serious operation is a shock for the entire system. I felt atrociously weak and ill. While I was led through the bellowing crowd of socialists to the rostrum, I was surprised to see the looks of violent hatred in the faces of some young men and women. If I hadn't been an invalid, I would surely have been attacked by them.

On election day, Churchill, along with his beloved wife, Clementine, closely followed the vote count. But the results were discouraging. Churchill was beaten by his Labour opponent by a difference of ten thousand votes.

A virtually forced retirement

Winston Churchill had been defeated at the polls and he also needed a time to rest, so on the spur of the moment he and Clementine decided to take a few days' holiday on the Riviera.

While in Cannes, he mainly spent his time painting.

He found painting to be an irresistible pleasure, since he was deeply attracted by the brilliant colours of the Côte d'Azur and could thus forget about his worries.

Churchill, then forty-eight years old, was in physical and personality terms as he has gone down in history. He played no sports, so physically he was not in especially good shape, plus he had a sweet tooth and loved wine and dining.

His way of dressing was a little extravagant. He always wore a bow tie, and he changed his shirt three times a day.

In fact, he was highly criticised, but he liked everyone to have at least something to say about him.

Churchill exhibited his paintings done on the Riviera in a Paris art gallery. Although they were signed using a pseudonym, they sold quite well and he earned about thirty thousand francs for them.

He gradually got back the energy he had lost because of his misfortune in the recent elections and the forced convalescence from his appendicitis operation.

In addition to painting, he also devoted himself to writing. In this case, the source of inspiration for his work was his memories of World War I, and this is how his work *The World Crisis* came to be published. In just a few weeks he finished the first of its five volumes. When the book appeared on the literary market, the entire first edition sold out immediately. This brought him almost twenty thousand pounds in profits, which he used to buy the family mansion, Chartwell Manor, a magnificent estate located in the county of Kent.

Finally, once totally recovered, he returned to England, having spent six months on the French Riviera instead of a few days.

CHAPTER XIV

CHANCELLOR OF THE EXCHEQUER

During the time Churchill spent in France, the political situation in England had undergone a few changes.

Bonar-Law, the leader of the Conservative Party and Prime Minister since the elections that had withdrawn Churchill from political life, had resigned. He was succeeded by Stanley Baldwin, another Conservative. But he had to call new elections, which were held in December 1923.

Churchill then found the occasion to return once again to political life. However, at that time the Liberals were in total disarray. He decided to run for the Leicester-West constituency as a Liberal candidate, but he was defeated by the Labour candidate. In fact, the new government cabinet was wholly Labour, since the Liberals were severely weakened in the elections and had to form a coalition with the Labour party in order to be able to govern. The King, who had to mediate in the matter, quite sportingly named Ramsey MacDonald of the Labour party to head the government. He was the new Prime Minister of a socialist government.

Of course, Churchill did not share the new ideas being bandied about, so he decided to write newspaper articles criticising the election of the government, which, he claimed, would completely subvert the country's social and economic structures.

Then, in a spectacular act, like so many others in his life, Churchill decided to run for the Conservative party in the new elections to ratify the government. He was no longer interested in the Liberals, since in addition to seeing no political future with them, they supported MacDonald without reservations.

He ran for the constituency of Westminster, but the party's central committee did not give him its support, and this led to a new defeat, although by a very small difference with the 'official' candidate backed by the Conservative party.

Churchill was encouraged. He knew that he was going along the right path and that it was just a matter of time before he would gain a seat as an MP or even a ministerial portfolio.

In October 1924 elections were held once again, caused by a crisis between Prime Minister MacDonald and the Liberals who supported his government. Churchill once again ran, although this time backed by the Conservative party.

The constituency chosen for the occasion was Epping, in Essex. And in these new elections he was elected representative for the House of Commons.

The Labour party had lost quite a few votes, although the Liberals were the ones that were truly defeated. Churchill had once again changed his loyalties at the right time.

In the new government, with Baldwin as Prime Minister, Churchill was most welcome. He was not assigned a portfolio, as he thought he would be, but the post offered him was that of Chancellor of the Exchequer.

He finally occupied the position that years earlier had belonged to his father.

During his five years in this office, things did not always go well for him, since, if truth be told, he did not understand much about finances.

Despite the fact that he had belonged to the Liberal party for quite a long time, Churchill actually, by ancestry and his own ideas, continued to be a conservative by nature. He held tight to certain strict values without realising that the war had brought about deep economic consequences. To him, the problem was reduced to whether the dollar had indeed relegated the pound sterling to second place, the only way of solving this was to return to the pre-war situation, so he convinced the government to return the pound sterling to the gold standard. If he had taken the time to listen to the new ideas that were emerging from economists at the time, he would have realised that what he was proposing would lead the country to an economic crisis.

Keynes had published a book entitled *The Economic Consequences of Peace*, and if Churchill had cared to peruse it he would have seen how mistaken his ideas were. But of course Keynes and his followers were leftists, and paying attention to the new Marxist-toned trends did not figure in Winston Churchill's mind.

When he heard about the Chancellor's economic policy, Keynes predicted its consequences, and he did not err in the least. In fact, the true consequence of Churchill's policy was that exports were more expensive. Churchill was wrong, and in 1925 the government, without much convincing, had to propose a reduction in wages so that production would be cheaper. The trade unions refused this proposal, and a general strike was convened for May 1926 which was to bring the whole country to a standstill for nine days.

But the government did not give in. The strike was ended by the trade unions, but the miners continued the conflict for six more months before accepting the conditions that were imposed: a 5% salary reduction and an extra half-hour added to the working day.

The strike cost England approximately eight hundred million pounds sterling. In addition, the working class was enraged with the Chancellor of the Exchequer. Keynes, for his part, published a new book entitled *The Economic Consequences of Mister Churchill*.

By 1928 the situation had not improved. There were more than one million unemployed persons registered at the unemployment offices. Likewise, English industry had to compete with other countries who had better technology: United States and Germany.

Finally, in 1928 the need was seen for new elections to be held.

The economic stagnation could only be ended by lowering the prices of English goods in order to recover the country's role as a major exporter. Two roads were possible: increasing productivity through technological modernisation, or reducing salaries. Since the former possibility could not be accomplished rapidly, Churchill inclined toward the latter, knowing that this would lead to a confrontation with the powerful labour unions. Churchill ignored the strike, supporting Premier Baldwin in declaring it illegal. This strength, this self-confidence in his own victory led the strikers (approximately 3,700,000) to go back to work, with the exception of the miners, who remained out of work for six months. However, the government's victory was Pyrrhic: production decreased and in 1929 England had to face the Great Depression with a million unemployed.

The claim that Great Britain had very limited industrial expansion before the 1929 crisis that should be revised, because in the face of the old industries the new ones arose in different geographical areas. Electricity began to be used as an alternative source of energy, which indicated an intense renewal of machinery. The capacity of the blast furnaces and steelworks also grew. In 1929 the shipbuilders managed to build half the ships in the world, and the concentration of the old cotton industry and the more modern chemical industry were taking place. Although it is true that the energy problems faced by England were serious, since coal was being left aside and this led to unemployment in the mining sector, the metallurgical industry appeared to be over-equipped and the shipbuilders had to orient their production toward to merchant marine after several years of only building warhsips.

CHAPTER XV

MEETING WITH MUSSOLINI

Winston Churchill, as we already know, was a man who liked getting involved in all issues related to government; one could even say that he always believed that everything should revolve around him and that – regardless of the post he occupied or even if he occupied no post – he believed that *he was the Government*.

Thus, during the time when he was Chancellor of the Exchequer, not only did he devote himself to finances, but because of his love of travel, he also got involved in foreign policy.

In 1927, on his way to Egypt for a short vacation, he stopped in Rome and paid a personal visit to Mussolini.

Churchill's declarations to the English press about the Italian fascist leader led to a series of scandals in both England and abroad. Churchill went so far as to say that the dictator had favourably impressed him, and that if he were Italian he would wholeheartedly support him in his battle against Leninism.

He was harshly criticised for his declarations, even by the Society of Nations. However, Churchill was not intimidated by this, rather he calmly continued on his trip to Egypt, where he spent his vacation painting landscapes and pyramids.

Another of his brilliants moves at this time was when in 1927 a search of the Soviet trade delegation in London disclosed that certain Russian civil servants were spies. At that time, Churchill was inflexible and managed to close the Russian embassy in London, and it remained closed for three years.

The Wall Street stock market crash

In 1928, as has already been said, it was considered necessary to call new elections. However, the English king's serious illness resulted in the politicians of all tendencies closing ranks.

In May 1929, Baldwin asked the king to dissolve the Parliament.

There was a new element in the elections this time: women over the age of twenty-one could vote for the first time, not only those over the age of thirty, as had been the rule until then.

The voting resulted in victory for the Labour party, while the Conservatives lost more than a hundred and fifty seats.

Despite this, Churchill was re-elected for the Epping constituency, although he was not able to form part of a government made up of trade unionists. The Conservatives, however, blamed Churchill for their defeat.

The result is that Churchill spent many more hours in Chartwell Manor, and that year he wrote *My Early Life*, a book that would be published in 1930.

He spent the rest of time in the House of Commons, in his opposition seat.

But 19th October 1929 has gone down in history as the day of the Wall Street crash in New York. That crash had repercussions around the world, and Britain was also affected.

The crisis in Britain began to be felt in 1930. The budget deficit reached unimaginable proportions, and not even foreign loans could cover the grave situation.

With his wife among the ruins of the London streets after a Nazi air raid in 1940.

On 24th August 1931 MacDonald presented his resignation. The King, aware of the gravity of the situation, convened the Liberal and Conservative leaders and asked them to form a new cabinet of national union. MacDonald then created a government in which Baldwin, the leader of the Conservative party, and Herbert Samuel, the leader of the Liberals, were the figureheads.

The new government's first decision was to suspend free convertibility of the pound sterling, thus expressing their censure of Churchill's economic policy. Obviously, Churchill was not asked to take on any portfolio.

He was re-elected for the Epping constituency when, following the custom, the political changes introduced were subject to a ratification vote by the people. But no one thought that Churchill would become important in English political life because it appeared that he would never again have the privilege of holding ministerial office.

The only people convinced that he would were Churchill himself and his wife, Clementine, who was unwavering in her constant support for him.

At that time, Churchill, taking refuge in literature, began to write one of the most extensive works that he ever published: the biography of his ancestor, the first Duke of Marlborough, John Churchill.

In Great Britain, the 1929 crisis arrived without any foreseeable solution along with the organisational crisis of the 1920s. Thus, the depression only served to corroborate the death throes of British world hegemony, which was already being challenged in the previous decade.

This changed had already been predicted by Siegfried in his book *The British Crisis in the 20th Century*: 'If we judge by its press, part of its elite, requests by its employers, labour unions and even some of its bankers, the moment will arrive for Britain to enter into a closed economic system".

To a large extent, Britain's withdrawal from its colonial empire was one of the consequences of the 1930s depression. In other words, Britain's loss of world power status went hand in hand with the decline of the pound sterling. The most important factor was, without a doubt, the increase in the trade deficit.

The capital exporting policy did not prove very sound. With this background, it is not surprising that from 1927 onwards many groups within the governing elite were considering the devaluation of the pound, the end of the free exchange rate and the creation of an imperial common market.

When in 1931 the crisis spread rapidly throughout Great Britain, these claims began to gain force. The balance of payments showed a deficit of 110 million pounds. At the end of July 1931, the loan that the Bank of England received from the Bank of France and the Federal Reserve was not capable of slowing down the withdrawal of funds from the City, and devaluation was imposed.

On 20th September 1931, Great Britain abandoned the gold standard and thus its convertibility into gold and, as mentioned above, a 25-30% devaluation was put into effect. This, then, was an acknowledgement that the United States had won the battle for financial leadership.

The monetary measures were immediately followed by customs innovations. Between November 1931 and February 1932, the adoption of protectionist measures ended almost a century of free trade. As a logical result, in August 1932 the Ottawa agreements established imperial preference. Great Britain and its dominions promised to lower their respective mutual trade tariffs. Great Britain likewise promised to buy certain amounts of agricultural products from its dominions. This was a strategy that provided immediate positive results. Production began to rise as of 1932, and in 1935 it almost reached 1929 levels, thanks to protectionist measures and the lower prices of imports, which led in turn to a lowering of the cost of living – 10% less than in 1929 – while salaries recovered 1929 levels and increased demand.

The Commonwealth, that is to say the former empire, had saved Great Britain once again.

CHAPTER XVI

DIM PROSPECTS

Churchill travelled to Germany in 1932 in order to study *in situ* the campaigns of his ancestor, the first Duke of Marlborough.

He who had virtually defined himself as a Germanophile in order to combat Bolshevism was shocked to discover incipient Nazism. He was not pleased with the fanatical Hitler youth. He began to realise the danger of Hitler.

In a speech given on the occasion of a German boycott of the Geneva Disarmament Conference, Churchill warned:

> *These young Teutons who go about Germany with the desire to sacrifice themselves for their fatherland shining in their eyes are not thinking about the parity of forces. They want weapons, and when they get them they will ask for the restitution of the colonies and lost territories. Please believe me: when these requests are made, the foundations of all the countries on Earth will be shaken.*

However, at that time, not much attention was paid to Churchill in the House of Commons. His speeches were met with indifference. The spirit of the English government was in favour of placating German demands, since it was believed that as the losers in the Great War they had the right to reproach and reclaim from the winners what had been theirs. It was felt that once their spirit was placated, the task of disarmament could once again be undertaken.

But Hitler was becoming an ever greater threat. In 1933 he came to power and, paradoxically, Churchill was then pleased that the USRR joined the Society of Nations. These reactions of Churchill's, which to the average observer could be defined as those of a man without very clear ideas, in reality were nothing more than a reaffirmation of the highly developed pragmatism of a man with a the gift of political foresight. Churchill did nothing more than study the palpable reality, and he acted as he saw fit on each occasion.

At that time, there were still few people who, like Churchill, had presentiments of the approaching tragedy.

But meanwhile, he remained quite removed from power. At that time, in 1935, at home in Chartwell Manor, he devoted himself to continuing work on his ancestor's biography and doing building work, dressed in a bricklayer's overall. Indeed, he became so skilful in handling the bricklayer's trowel that he even joined the national Bricklayer's Union.

At the same time, in 1935, Britain was also celebrating the twenty-fifth anniversary of the reign of George V and Queen Mary.

Almost at the same time, Ramsay MacDonald withdrew from political life and Baldwin was named Prime Minister. His ratification by means of a popular referendum resulted in the Conservative party gaining the most votes, with the Labour party coming in second. The Liberals were left totally out of the race. Churchill was elected for his constituency once again.

In autumn 1935, Churchill, as always accompanied by Clementine, his personal secretary and a servant, went off for a holiday in North Africa, specifically to Marrakech, where he wished to rest and especially to paint.

In 1935, too, Mussolini wanted to take possession of Ethiopia. Italy already had under its dominion Libya, Eritrea and Somalia. The fascist troops were taking up position along the Ethiopian border. There was unanimous reprobation of Mussolini by Britain and the Society of Nations. But on 5 October the Italian troops crossed the Ethiopian border and, despite the fact that the Society of Nations' Security Council decided to apply collective sanctions against Italian fascism, Mussolini's troops continued to advance in their conquest of Ethiopian territory.

When 1935 came to an end, the following year arrived in Britain under a dark cloud. On 20th January, King George V died. His successor, Edward VIII, only reigned for three hundred days.

Edward VIII's abdication

The elder son of the deceased King George, the former Prince of Wales, Edward Albert Patrick David, succeeded his father on the throne with the name of Edward VIII.

The king's romance with the American, Wallis Simpson, was public knowledge. She was awaiting divorce from her second husband. However, all the indications were that once he was on the throne, Edward would reconsider his posture and take some woman of royal blood as his wife. But Edward VIII, pressured by the Prime Minister, chose abdication rather than renounce his love for Wallis.

Churchill, a close friend of the King, used all his means to put off the abdication as long as possible, but he did not succeed. Churchill was especially fond of the new King, since he had known him since they were children and held him in high esteem. The only thing he could do for the monarch was to help him put the finishing touches to his abdication speech, which Edward read over the radio to bid the nation farewell.

The outgoing King abdicated in favour of his brother, the Duke of York, one year younger than himself, who reigned as George VI.

The new King's coronation ceremony took place on 17 May 1937 in Westminster, and Churchill, who at that time was merely an MP, was not able to attend the coronation.

Churchill against Hitler

On the other hand, Churchill had once again fallen into disfavour for having taking Edward VIII's side when the House called for his abdication.

Shortly before, when Hitler had invaded the Rhineland, in French territory, he had been heeded with great attention. Indeed, on 7th March 1936, Hitler, in a speech broadcast from the Reichstag in Berlin, had announced to the people that the Wehrmacht was going to take possession of the Rhineland.

France felt vulnerable before the prospect of that invasion since English public opinion was indifferent and virtually on Hitler's side, the contrary, of course, of Churchill, who saw World War II coming. However, Churchill mistook the dates, since he thought that the conflict would begin between 1937 and 1938. By that time, Churchill's speeches were being heeded more and more. But his having appealed on Edward VIII's behalf had once again relegated him to secondary status.

Then, since Churchill no longer had anything to lose, he wholeheartedly devoted himself to the cause of European peace, based on opposing Hitler, and he incessantly gave speeches before a government that was mostly concerned about gaining their electors' votes by the favourite avenue, pacifism.

Winston Churchill defended the alliance with France. He began to actively get involved in a Franco-English association, continually pressuring the government of his country to attempt to dissuade Italy from forming a block with Germany. Furthermore, he was determined to include the Soviet Union in the fight against Nazism.

Meanwhile, Prime Minister Stanley Baldwin, tired and ageing, decided to withdraw from politics. He was succeeded by the man who until then had been Chancellor of the Exchequer, Neville Chamberlain.

Churchill's relations with Chamberlain were cordial, but the moment had not yet arrived for him to once again hold office in the government.

Thus, he remained devoted to fighting against Hitler and especially to finishing off the great biography of his ancestor. At that time, he was sixty-three years old, and his vitality and intelligence were at their peak, just as in his youth. Aware of everything happening in the world, he always based his judgements on a knowledge of the facts. He understood perfectly well that a new international conflict was going to break out shortly in Europe and that England was going to have to fight just like any other nation, not only with the force of weapons but also with the strength of spirit in order not to fall into the dishonour of forsaking a morally respectable civilisation.

It is worth recalling the speech that he gave in March 1938 after German troops invaded Austria. The lines below are a small excerpt, but they serve as a sample to help us understand his position:

> *Austria has been invaded by Nazism. The gravity of this event should not and cannot be underestimated since Europe is facing a plan of aggression which has been carefully and rigorously developed, and measured and executed down to the detail. England can only choose between submission or the immedi-*

ate adoption of measures that will either eliminate the danger or if not, confront it properly.

But the vast majority of people only managed to see the Nazi invasion as the logical merger of two twin nations that had been separated only by borders, but that even shared the same language.

Chamberlain, the great defender of peace, exhausted his resources in his attempts to ignore provocation by Hitler who, after Austria, made it clear that his next objective would be Czechoslovakia.

Sir Arthur Neville, better known as Chamberlain, had been born in Edgbaston, Birmingham, in 1869. He was elected Conservative MP in 1918 and had performed different roles within the government in which he proved himself to be an excellent administrator. He was one of Baldwin's main associates, and he was behind the 1924 reunification of the Conservative party. In 1931 he was appointed Chancellor of the Exchequer. In the fight against a very negative set of circumstances, he led the state in the task of readjusting the British economy and participated in developing the Ottawa agreements (1932), which in the end enacted one of the favourite projects of his father, Joseph Chamberlain. In 1937 he succeeded Baldwin as Prime Minister. While he stressed the urgency to rearm, Churchill attempted to keep the peace as long as possible, ceding in claims that seemed to be justifiable. In September 1938, when the German-Czech crisis broke out, he channelled all his efforts to achieving a reconciliation. He met with Hitler in Berchtesgarden and Godesberg, and signed the famous Munich Pact (29-30th September).

The liquidation of Czechoslovakia in 1939, while brutally altering the balance so painstakingly achieved, meant the failure of his policy. From then on, preparations for resistance to the German expansion sped up, and he immediately signed a guarantee treaty with Poland (which in the end was inoperable due to a lack of agreement with the USSR). When the German troops invaded Poland he declared war on Germany. But his government was overwhelmed by the early German successes, and in May 1940 he turned over the stewardship of the country to Winston Churchill.

When Prime Minister Chamberlain signed the Munich Pact, Churchill had declared that England had suffered "a total and unmitigated defeat". His words were met with jeers, like those of a war-monger who wanted to ruin the general joy at peace. But one year later, events proved him to be right: Hitler's troops invaded Poland in their thirst for more territory, and war broke out, the most destructive war known to date.

Talking about Chamberlain in Munich, Churchill commented that he knew nothing about Europe, but that he had an excess of self-confidence, which led him to take risks that put the country at risk. "His only ambition was to go down in history as the author of peace. He was forging war when all he wanted was the opposite".

Chamberlain's supporters insisted on stating that what he did in his negotiations with Hitler was buy time so that the democracies could rearm. That is not so clear. But France, with Prime Minister Edouard Deladier at the helm, was also responsible for the outcome, although in his defence it must be said that Deladier had behind him a poorly armed country, militant pacifism and an extreme right-wing 'fifth column' that was provoking a crisis of democracy.

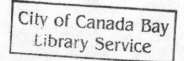

CHAPTER XVII

THE EVENTS LEADING UP TO
WORLD WAR II

It was clear that Hitler was planning to invade Czechoslovakia. In 1925, France had signed a treaty of mutual assistance with Czechoslovakia: if Germany attacked it, France had to rapidly intervene in the matter. But England had no commitment to Czechoslovakia. The Treaty of Locarno only specified that it would support France if the latter were attacked by Germany. France alone could not oppose a Germany that was better armed than it was.

During the second half of May 1938, tensions along the Czech border increased considerably. Hitler was on the lookout for any pretext for crossing the border.

The British government at that time sent a communiqué to France in which Britain's desire to remain neutral in case of a conflict was made clear, adding that everything possible had been done by the path of negotiation and that warnings had even been sent to the German government that they were sure would not be ignored. And it added that the French government should not overestimate the scope of the British warnings to Germany, since it would not intervene in the matter.

This made Churchill despair. From that moment on he continued to denounce even more vehemently the danger of Nazism, and he became frustrated because he had no influence over the men in power.

On 15th September, aware of the gravity of the situation, Chamberlain went to Germany to meet with Hitler. He was received cordially, but when Chamberlain attempted to dissuade him from his intentions in Czechoslovakia, Hitler appealed to the rights of peoples and especially the self-determination of the German minorities, so that he claimed what he considered belonged to Germany: annexation of the Sudetenland by the Reich.

Once back in England, Chamberlain was convinced that the only solution to Czechoslovakia and to keep the peace was to cede to the dictator's wishes, in the hopes that this would be his last demand. And he thus proposed this, presenting the Czech government with the Godesberg Memorandum, which specified the cession to the Third Reich of the territories inhabited by a German-speaking majority. Naturally, the Czech government was exasperated by this proposition, but the general opinion was that nothing else could be done but acquiesce to it with resignation, since France also supported Chamberlain's proposal.

An irreversible process was then triggered. Both Poland and Hungary then claimed part of Czech territory where they also had ethnic minorities. Adolf Hitler demanded the immediate occupation of the Sudetenland by his troops. Chamberlain once again met with Hitler in Godesberg on the 22nd of the same month and attempted to negotiate, since in Prague, Eduardo Benes had formed a new government that had rejected the Godesberg Memorandum. However, the German dictator was inflexible.

The day before Chamberlain's second trip to Godesberg, Churchill gave a speech which had a great impact and aroused serious controversies. He criticised the fact that the policy adopted by England and France would bring about the capitulation of the Western democracies to Nazi demands. He especially emphasised that this stance would not lead to peace,

A 1940 propaganda poster.

but quite to the contrary, it would bring much more danger-ous situations to the European nations and would weaken them:

> *The dismemberment of Czechoslovakia under the pressure of England and France is equivalent to complete capitulation by the Western democracies to the Nazi threat. But this submission, far from bringing peace and security to England and France, will to the contrary put them in a situation of weakness that is even more dangerous.*

As a result of this speech by Churchill, political circles started to realise that peace at any price was not the best course of action.

At that time, Spain was living the last throes of its Republic under fire from Italian and German troops, while England continued with its non-interventionist policy.

Churchill travelled to Paris, and when he returned to London on 26th September, he began to pressure Chamberlain to assume an attitude of solidarity with France, which was being forced into conflict because of the pact it had signed with Prague years earlier.

The following day, Chamberlain announced on the radio that much against his will he would undertake offensive action if any nation attempted to dominate the world using the force of arms. Hitler, in reply, decided to mobilise the Wehrmacht, while France and England were experiencing tense moments: the Royal Navy was on stand-by; in London gas masks were being distributed, and the French and British governments were in constant contact.

The final supreme effort to keep peace came from Georges Bonnet, who on the night of the 27-28th September, ordered the French ambassador in Berlin to talk to Hitler while he himself tried to contact Mussolini.

On 21st September 1938, Churchill made the following declaration to the London press:

> The dismemberment of Czechoslovakia by virtue of pressure from England and France equals a complete surrender of the Western democracies to the Nazis' threats to use force. Such a collapse will bring neither peace nor security to England or France. On the contrary, it will place both nations in an ever weaker and more dangerous situation. The mere neutralisation of Czechoslovakia means leaving 25 German divisions free to threaten the western front. In addition, the path to the Black Sea will be left wide open for the triumphant Nazis. Not only is Czechoslovakia threatened, but also democracy and freedom for all nations. It is a fatal deception to think that security can be gained by throwing a small state to the wolves. Germany's war potential will soon grow at a faster rate than France and Great Britain will be able to complete their defence measures.

On the French minister Bonnet's mission, Churchill would later write in his *Memoirs*:

> Many of us, even in the ministries, had the impression that Bonnet epitomised the quintessence of defeatism and that all his skilful verbal manoeuvres had no purpose other than to grasp at peace at any price.

> Bonnet was attempting, after all, to paint Chamberlain and our Foreign Minister, Lord Halifax,

as the culprits. But there can be no doubt about what he really thought. He wanted to elude compliance with France's solemn, needed and recently renewed obligations to go to war in defence of Czechoslovakia at any cost. The governments of France and England seemed then like two overripe melons smashed against each other at a time when what was needed was to make the weapons of steel glisten. Everyone was in agreement on one thing: there should be no discussion about what their "guardians" decided. It was impossible to imagine a worse way to proceed.

CHAPTER XVIII

THE MUNICH PACT

In a desperate act, Chamberlain asked for Mussolini's intervention, at the same time that the French ambassador in Berlin asked Hitler for a meeting with Chamberlain and Daladier. Hitler accepted, and thus the following day, 29th September, Chamber and Deladier went to Munich, where Mussolini would join them.

That night a pact was signed, without Czech participation, which consisted of nothing more and nothing less than the dismemberment of Czechoslovakia, since it was foreseen that in early October the German troops would occupy the Sudetenland while waiting for a plebiscite for an international commission to decide on the permanent borders.

Chamberlain was convinced that he had peacefully resolved the problem and returned to London triumphantly.

Winston Churchill, however, believed that, far from a triumph, the only thing that had been achieved was a crushing defeat. Finally, his repeated speeches against Chamberlain's policy ended up having an effect on the government, and by the end of 1938 the aeronautic industries were working against the clock. In France, arms production was also stepped up.

Winston Churchill had been right when he prophesised the worst. Not only was the Sudetenland occupied, but the districts of Teschen and Frystat were turned over to Poland.

Hungary, too, was given nearly five thousand square miles of Czech territory.

At the end of the month of January 1939, in a speech Hitler proclaimed a German colonial empire and made known his total support for Mussolini, who claimed Tunisia, Corsica and Nice.

In March of the same year, the Wehrmacht entered Prague. On the 24th of that month, Churchill wrote:

> *The aggression we so feared has come about. Adolf Hitler is following step by step the process he set forth in Mein Kampf, and in doing so he has broken the ties of good faith that bind the British and French statesmen, who had believed his word. The Munich Pact has been brutally violated, despite the many advantages it held for Germany. Germany cannot be trusted again while it continues under its current masters. People's feelings and opinions have changed, and this will spread throughout all the dominions.*

Once again, Churchill was right. When the Danzig crisis broke, Hitler only succeeded in worsening, if possible, the already awful opinion the British had of him, as they were extremely upset by the way their Prime Minister had been hoaxed.

France had the same agreement with Poland that it had with Czechoslovakia, but Great Britain had no commitment to Warsaw. Thus, the situation was the same as it had been with the Czechs. Now, however, the British stance had changed considerably. On 31st March in the House of Commons, Chamberlain gave a speech that indicated that France and Great Britain would join together if Poland were attacked. Likewise, at Churchill's suggestion, they would try to gain the support of the Soviet Union in the fight against Hitler, but this attempt was not successful.

Quite to the contrary, in August the German Minister of Foreign Affairs signed a German-Soviet pact with his colleague, Molotov, in Moscow. The pact established the neutrality of both nations if one of them were attacked by a foreign power. In addition, a ten-year commitment to non-aggression was signed in the document.

For his part, at that time Churchill was the lightning rod for public opinion. The political media recognised that he had been right from the start, and there were some street demonstrations demanding he occupy a post in the government.

On 24th August, Roosevelt appealed to Victor Manuel III, Hitler and Moscicki, President of Poland, to begin direct negotiations between Poland and Germany, or to allow a third power to mediate between then.

In an extraordinary session, the English Parliament approved the allocation of full powers to the English government, and also signed a mutual aid pact with Poland.

The following day, Hitler asked the British ambassador for freedom of action in his conflict, and on the 29th he reiterated his territorial claims on Danzig and refused to negotiate if his claims were not met.

On the morning of 1st September, German troops entered Poland.

England was ready to take action. However, action was not taken soon because first an ultimatum was sent at the express request of France, demanding that Hitler withdraw his troops from Polish soil. However, the ultimatum, which was sent to the German ambassador on 3rd September, only granted two hours for the withdrawal of German troops. Thus, on 3rd September at 11 a.m. Great Britain went to war.

111

At the end of World War I, Danzig, an ancient city of the Germanic peoples, at the behest of the victors, became the capital of a tiny state, whose territory (760 square miles) is like a wedge between Poland's corridor to the sea and the German territory of East Prussia. Formally, the state was formerly 'free under the protection of the Society of Nations', but in practice it was controlled by Poland, which imposed a customs union on it. Of its 412,000 inhabitants (256,000 lived in Danzig), 75% were German, as were 90% of the residents of the capital.

After Hitler's rise to power, the local Nazi party, led by Forster, won the local elections in 1937 and established a totalitarian regime.

During the 1930s, western public opinion was convinced that the existence of the Polish corridor and the Danzig enclave was absurd and a threat to world peace, which was in line with Hitler's strategy. Both Chamberlain and Deladier felt inclined to pacify Berlin by turning Danzig over to it, so that they pressured Poland, and the call resounded in the French parliament.

The war began in Danzig a few hours before the German troops crossed the Polish border, with the shelling of the Westerplatte by the cruiser *Schleswig-Holstein*; but the Poles valiantly resisted in the square itself despite the superior number of enemy troops. Only in the final hours of 7th September did the Nazis from the interior manage to take over the city.

According to Hitler and his Staff, despite French and British declarations, world war was still avoidable. British aircraft had not yet made an appearance in German air space, and the navy remained in its ports. The French army guarded the Maginot line, beyond which only a few carefully chosen raids were made that did very little to avert the imminent Polish defeat. The inability of the democracies to react seemed clear. Was it still possible to reach an agreement with the Western powers? Would Great Britain, taking refuge in its 'splendid island isolation', end up reaching an agreement with Berlin?

CHAPTER XIX
WORLD WAR II

That Sunday, 3rd September, the House of Commons met. Chamberlain was downcast. His efforts toward keeping the peace had been in vain. However, when Chamberlain finished speaking, Churchill gave an encouraging speech to the Prime Minister in which he claimed to feel comforted by living in a country where younger generations were willing to demonstrate that they were worthy of those men who had built the greatness of the nation.

When the plenary session ended, Churchill was called by Prime Minister Chamberlain and was informed by him that he was going to constitute a restricted War Cabinet in which he had decided that Churchill would take part as First Lord of the Admiralty.

That same night a radio signal was broadcast to all the navies with only three words: "Winston is back".

After lunching that day at his daughter Sarah's house, Winston Churchill went quickly to the Admiralty and, from that moment on he began to act in an unusual way for a man about to turn sixty-five. He worked tirelessly, so much so that he even decided to move into the Admiralty building itself. Clementine lived in chambers that served as their home at the time. She moved some furniture from their house and Churchill had telephones installed everywhere, in order to remain in permanent contact with all the branches of the Ministry and the fleet.

On 1st October, Churchill gave a radio speech to the entire country. His words left no room for doubt: he was convinced, as he would be throughout the war, that England would win. In fact, he knew that the civil population needed encouragement, and thus arose the most important sentences of his talk:

> *Hitler has begun the war when he wanted. But it will not end until we are quite sure that he has received what he deserves.*

The First Lord of the Admiralty was also convinced that one of the most important weapons in that conflagration was propaganda. Thus, every time a victory at sea was achieved by sinking a German ship, the news was exploited to the maximum. One example of this was the splendid ceremony for the crews of the cruisers *Exeter* and *Ajax* when they returned to England after attacking the German battleship *Graf von Spee* near Montevideo until the captain of the German ship decided to sink it and then commit suicide. Not only did many people attend that ceremony, but the King and Queen were also in attendance.

In addition, Churchill personally inspected the ships at the naval bases and even personally supervised the air forces. He was always accompanied by his wife, and by doing so she instilled courage into the wives the soldiers and officers wives.

After the destruction of the House of Commons in 1941.

CHAPTER XX

CHURCHILL IS NAMED PRIME MINISTER

At the beginning of the month of December 1939, after seizing the Baltic countries, the Soviet Union invaded Finland. Despite the fact that it was facing a giant like the USSR, this small country put up a fierce resistance. For some months the continental newspapers were full of news and photographs of the fierce battle taking place in this small, snowy country. In the end, Finland could not hold out, and in March 1940 the Helsinki government was forced to negotiate with the USSR.

France and England were harshly criticised for not having helped the Finns. In France, Deladier had to resign and hand over his position to Paul Reynaurd, to Churchill's great glee, since he was Reynaurd's good friend and considered him a decisive, intrepid man. He was not wrong, since on his own and to his own risk, without checking with the president of the country, in London he signed a commitment with England that joined them in both war and peace. The commitment was drafted in the following terms:

> *The governments of the French Republic and Great Britain and Northern Ireland promise not to negotiate nor reach any armistice or peace treaty during the war unless it is by mutual agreement. Likewise they promise not to debate the terms of peace before unanimous agreement between them on the condi-*

tions needed to assure the respective guarantees for their security. Finally, they promise to maintain their society of action in any field once the war is over, for as long as necessary, to safeguard their security and be able to rebuild, just like other nations, an international order that guarantees freedom for the people, respect for the law and the preservation of peace in Europe.

Criticism poured onto the British Prime Minister, Chamberlain, for having signed that very agreement, which bound Great Britain not only during the war, but also once it was over, but he was able to face up to this criticism well. However, he could no longer deal with the members of the House of Commons after the failure that took place on the Norwegian coasts in May 1940.

Churchill had planned to cut the route of German supplies of Swedish iron ore, for which the German ships had necessarily to pass through the Norwegian port of Narvik. In early April, specifically on the 8th, a French-English operation was begun involving mining the entry to the port of Narvik. However, it appears that the Germans were aware of the operation and on the 9th, without prior warning, they made a air attack over the Sea of Norway.

The English fleet began to attack the German fleet, and thus began three major naval battles with favourable results-for the allies, who were able to land two expeditionary corps: one on an island facing Narvik, where twenty thousand men landed, and the other in the towns of Andalsnes and Namsos, on either side of the port of Trondheim, where three thousand troops landed. The German counterattack was extremely fierce, and at the end of April the allies had to give up their positions in Andalsnes and Namsos.

The members of the House of Commons demanded responsibilities for that defeat and they asked for Chamberlain's resignation. After this issue was debated and later voted, although he still achieved a small majority, because of the negative votes of the members of his own party Chamberlain chose to offer the leader of the Labour Party the opportunity to form a coalition government: However, Attlee refused, as he had done at the beginning of the war. Chamberlain was then obliged to present his resignation to the King, and the monarch then ordered Churchill to form a coalition in which he would act as Prime Minister.

Everyone in England was convinced that if anyone could hold the reins of government, it was Churchill. His destiny was finally about to come true. He was almost sixty-six years old.

Winston Churchill quickly formed his cabinet. This time Attlee agreed to take part, as did Sinclair, the leader of the Liberal party. Anthony Eden, Churchill's personal friend, took on the portfolio of the War Ministry. Chamberlain was offered the honorary position of Lord President of the Council. And Churchill himself took on the Defence portfolio.

At that time, Churchill knew that just like all the other allies, England was on the verge of catastrophe. The responsibility was very heavy and there were few possibilities of rallying the nation from its slump, both physical and moral.

The German armies were quite superior to the allies in all respects. When Hitler began his campaign in the west after dividing the conquered Poland with the USSR, he had 2,439 modern-style tanks, compared with France's 2,460 and England's mere 229, of which 171 were mini-tanks. Forces were apparently closely balanced between German and French tanks, but the facts proved the opposite to be true. German theory on the use of tanks was far superior to French. The mobility of the German tanks was incredible because their efficiency lay in independent armoured divisions employing an effective battering ram tactic, while the French strategy for the distribution of tanks was based on infantry support.

In the air, German aviation was unquestionably superior, since it had entered into the campaign with 3,700 combat planes and more than 600 transport planes, while the French air force only had 1,500 planes. The Belgian and Dutch air forces were scant, and since Churchill's advice to reinforce the Royal Air Force had not been heeded, the English air force only had 474 planes based in France, with the rest – not even half that many – remaining in England.

When Churchill appeared before the House of Commons to account for the new government, he did so energetically, and he began by giving a speech that the entire nation would hear. A true portrait of the man can be drawn from this speech:

> *I cannot tell the House more than what I have told the men that have agreed to form part of the government: I can only offer you blood, sweat and tears. We are facing the most serious of trials and we must face many long months of fighting and suffering. But our goal shall be this: Victory! Victory, whatever the cost! I accept the obligation set before me, totally sure that the cause shall not be lost, but I have the right to ask for everyone's participation, and thus I tell you: Come and let us march together!*

Discouraging news came trickling into London. The Germans had invaded Belgium, Luxembourg and the Netherlands, and their next objective was to invade France.

The invasion of France

On 5th June the Battle of the Somme began. In only five days it would end in disaster, and Churchill, summoned by the French, travelled to Paris. The French government asked Churchill to send all his anti-aircraft reinforcements to France. But he refused, claiming that the moment had not yet arrived, and that he had to use all means to attempt to keep control over English territory in order to re-conquer France. The conference with the French lasted two days, but no viable conclusion was reached. Both Petain and Weygand were willing to capitulate. And so they did. Churchill returned to London, and on the 14th the Germans entered Paris.

Reynaud's government resigned. Lebrun then called Pétain and ordered him to form a new government. It was decided to ask London to break the pact Reynaud had signed in order to ask for the terms for an armistice. London accepted, not without first sending a generous offer in which France and England would cease to be two separate nations and would become the Franco-British Union. But the French government believed that it was too late for this and preferred to surrender.

On 18th June, while the French government waited in Bordeaux for the German answer, from London General De Gaulle encouraged the French to unite and continue the fight.

On 22nd June, the Pétain government signed the armistice. England remained alone facing an enemy that now occupied the entire north of Europe.

CHAPTER XXI

THE WAR IN GREAT BRITAIN

England was totally alone against the enemy. Churchill began to think about his friend, Roosevelt, but the Japanese attack on Pearl Harbor had to occur before the Americans would join the war.

In the battle that Great Britain was going to face against Germany, Churchill only had two ways of winning: first, the quality of the Royal Air Force and the resistance it could put up against the Luftwaffe, despite the fact that the German air force had many more planes; and second, the possibility that the naval fleet could keep the waters open and could thus maintain communications with the Commonwealth. The English naval fleet in 1940 was superior to the German fleet, although there existed the possibility that Hitler would use the French fleet for his purposes.

Thus, understandably, as condition for France's signing the armistice Churchill had stipulated that it would order the French fleet to English ports.

However, the armistice was requested before the fate of the fleet was decided in Bordeaux, and once the negotiations had begun it was impossible to undertake any action that could be interpreted by the victors as betrayal.

When signing the armistice, Hitler had promised not to use the French fleet for his own war operations. But one had to be armed with very strong faith in order to believe the dictator. Thus, Churchill decided that the best course of action would be to destroy as many vessels in the French fleet as possible. And he ordered this to take palce. Thus began Operation Catapult, which was established on Churchill's personal orders in order to capture and destroy all French war vessels wherever they happened to be located.

Some of the French warships were in the ports of Portsmouth and Plymouth, and their crews were forcefully disembarked and forced to join the English marine corps. Meanwhile, in Alexandria a French fleet in the port consisting of a battleship, four cruisers, three torpedo-launchers and a submarine was partially disarmed on an amicable basis.

But the real tragedy took place at Mers El-Kebir, where part of the French fleet there was warned to head toward Great Britain or American ports. Faced with the fleet admiral's refusal, Churchill personally gave the order to attack and four French war vessels were sunk. As a result of this operation, about one thousand three hundred French sailors were declared dead or missing.

Churchill knew that there would be resentment toward this operation in France; however, it was quite clear that the English would not be easily beaten and that, to the contrary, they would put up stiff resistance to the enemy.

The German attack

Invading France had taken Hitler no more than six weeks. The Führer had planned to end with the French Republic in four months, and now he had plenty of time on his hands. He had not yet planned how to launch the attack against the English, and this would prove to be decisive, since Churchill was well able to take advantage of this situation.

Great Britain had at its disposal all the planes that it had decided not to sacrifice shortly before, as it viewed that the battle for France was lost, and now they were all prepared to face the enemy. Radar stations for detecting Luftwaffe positions were now rapidly installed.

When on 8th August 1940 Goering ordered that the island be attacked, the Royal Air Force was able to fight back valiantly.

The attack lasted ten days, during which the German bombers met with coastal defence fire as soon as they were picked up by the radar. And when they managed to overcome the coastal barrier they met with the brave pilots of the Hurricanes and Spitfires who courageously fought to defend English air space.

After those terrible ten days had passed, it could be seen that despite the fact that the Channel ports had been partially destroyed, the RAF continued to rule the air, although there had been numerous casualties amongst the pilots who had gone down during fighting. But the German air force was the real loser, and it had had to make a hasty retreat in order to regroup. More than seven hundred German planes had been destroyed.

On 20th August Churchill knew that he had won a battle but not the war, and that the German army would continue attacking until it beat them or else succumbed in the attempt. Thus, Winston Churchill worked tirelessly for a man his age: he sent orders and instructions that had to be followed in case of invasion, and he even personally oversaw air base and army unit inspections.

At the end of July, the plan for how to meet invasion was perfectly defined. On 7th September recognisance planes warned that all types of enemy troops were gathering from Ostende to Le Havre.

The heaviest air raids that the English people were to suffer then began. German planes especially targeted the civilian population. City residents had to take refuge in bomb shelters and left them only when the air raid sirens sounded the all clear.

The atrocious bombings by the Germans angered Churchill more than anyone, and he always protested when he had to enter a shelter. On this matter, one of his associates claimed that when Churchill was in a bomb shelter he was so impatient that he ended up being more dangerous than the German bombs themselves.

The story is told that one of those nights that seemed more like a nightmare than reality, during the course of an extremely long drawn-out raid, Churchill went up onto the roof of a house and sat there to watch the spectacle with an unlit cigar in his mouth. A few minutes later the district head came to tell Churchill that he was sitting on top of the air shaft and that the people inside were suffocating.

It appears that the Prime Minister was fascinated by the spectacle of the exploding bombs, and another night, when he was at the door of 10 Downing Street, his bodyguard, Sergeant W. H. Thompson from Scotland Yard, had to keep reminding him that that house, being the customary residence of the Prime Ministers of the British government, was a true death trap.

The bombs dropped by the German air force never managed to hit Churchill, but he remained in constant personal danger. Among other measures taken to ensure the Prime Minister's safety, the government ordered anti-aircraft weapons to be installed at Chequers, the country home of the British prime ministers, as well as at Chartwell, Winston Churchill's family estate, where he sometimes spent a few days working, since it had been discovered that both houses were the favourite target of the German planes, who flew over at a low altitude in their desire to put an end to Hitler's staunchest enemy.

At the Tehran Conference along with Stalin in November 1943.

Day after day, from 7th September on, the German air raids would make steel and fire rain down on the people of London.

But Great Britain's fighting spirit resided in its aviation. Churchill even ordered a uniform of commodore of the Royal Air Force and visited all the bases. He also found the time to give speeches in the House of Commons and speak to the British people on the radio.

Through all of 1940, an invasion was expected. The General Defence Headquarters was prepared to send out the agreed signal – *Cromwell* – but tensions began to die down at the beginning of October, since the Luftwaffe had lost more than two thousand planes in the Battle of Britain, which they would sorely miss when they decided to cross the Straits of Dover.

Meanwhile, Churchill stepped up his relations with Roosevelt, who had been re-elected President of the United States for the third time in November. On 29th December 1940 Roosevelt declared that his country had to become the great arsenal of democracy, and one week later he got Congress to pass a law called "Lend and Lease", in which the President of the U.S. was authorised to have domestic production at his disposal for any foreign country whose defence was seen as necessary for the protection of the United States.

In this way, Churchill was assured a steady source of supplies from the United States. But despite the good prospects, a series of disasters struck one after another. While the German air raids on London continued every night, the Mediterranean basin fell into the hands of the Axis.

Hitler sent the Afrika Korps to help Mussolini, and shortly after the invasion of Yugoslavia began, which then continued on to Greece. Hitler triumphed in the Balkans while the British army had to fall back in Egypt.

And Britain's misfortunes were not over yet. The British army had to face Rommel, who was in charge of the Afrika

Corps. Rommel managed to repel Wawell east of the Egyptian border, leaving Cairo and Alexandria under imminent threat.

However, Churchill remained imperturbable and full of energy, convinced that Great Britain would emerge victorious from that cruel war.

Who was the so-called 'Desert Fox'? Erwin Johannes Eugen Rommel was one of the few German generals who gained respect and popularity both in his country and in the enemies of the Third Reich. Born in 1891 to a family in Württemberg with no military background – his father and grandfather had been teachers – in 1910 he began a career which would lead him to be a Field Marshall and one of the geniuses of armoured conflict. After his baptism of fire in World War I, he taught in several military academies. When World War II began, he was commander of the Führer's military guard.

An officer with a notable professional military spirit and without ideological nor political notions, in February 1940 Rommel gained a position at the front line as a commander of the 7th Panzer division, with which he headed the German advance in Belgium and northern France. He soon became the symbol of a front-line general in German public opinion, a factor which was exploited by the Reich's propaganda machine, so that he was even presented as a figure from the Nazi party, which in fact he never joined.

On the European front, Rommel developed his essential knowledge of modern motorised warfare, when he discovered the tactical possibilities of tanks and mobile artillery as offensive weapons in a war of movements. In February 1941 this led the Führer to name him head of the flamboyant Afrika Korps, which was sent to support the Italian troops in the Libyan desert.

The favourable North African desert terrain allowed Rommel to develop his brilliant tactical abilities in tank warfare to the full. For three years the 'Desert Fox' would surprise the British with a daring campaign and 'clean warfare' that made him popular even among enemy ranks.

At that time, although his prestige in Germany was rising and he was promoted to the rank of Field Marshal, his problems with the Third Reich's political apparatus were beginning. His army would reach Tobruk victorious, but Berlin ignored his requests for reinforcements and fuel. His troops had given their all and the heroic and decisive defeat at El.Alamein in November 1942 was an honour for him and all his troops. In May 1943 Germany would lose all of North Africa to the allies. Rommel would then lead the German forces in Italy.

In 1944 Rommel became head of the Atlantic defence on the Normandy coast when Germany already realised that the war was lost. He was on the brink several times, but after being seriously injured in a British air raid, he finally agreed to join the conspirators against the Führer without knowing that the key to the plot lay in assassinating Hitler. The plot failed and his ties to it became known. On 14th October 1944 the Gestapo made the loyal general take a dose of poison. Berlin buried him with military honours and covered up his role in the rebellion against Hitler. Upon peace, his widow was invited to England by the English authorities, recalling that tenacious but chivalrous enemy.

CHAPTER XXII

GERMANY INVADES THE USSR

On dawn on 22nd June 1941, Hitler, betraying the German-Soviet agreement signed by Molotov and Von Ribbentrop on 23rd August 1939, launched an invasion of the Soviet Union.

Churchill was not surprised by this development. He expected something like this from the German dictator, and this gave England the opportunity of no longer being alone in the fight against the German army. On 10th July 1941, with the representative from the USSR, Great Britain signed an agreement with the Russian representative under which Britain and the Soviet Union promised not to negotiate a separate peace.

Churchill made a speech over the radio on the Wehrmacht's invasion of the Soviet Union, in which he denounced the German aggression and repeated England's war aims, which may be summarised in fighting the Nazis and their allies on land, sea and air:

> *Every man and every state that combats the Nazi dictatorship shall have our support, just as any man or any state that supports it shall be our enemy. Thus, it is logical to deduce that we shall provide all the help we can to the Soviet Union. We will also ask our allies and friends around the world to adopt the same policy. This is not a class war but an armed conflict in which Great Britain and the Commonwealth are involved,*

133

without distinctions of race, creed or political party.
The danger threatening the USSR is our danger as well,
and that of the United States, as is the cause of all
Russians who fight to defend their home and their home-
land. It is the cause of all men all over the planet.

According to German propaganda, Hitler was advancing directly toward Moscow. However, despite the fact that the German dictator had thought he only needed three weeks to reach the Soviet capital, in the middle of the month of July the first assault wave was virtually stopped in its tracks. However, by the end of July Hitler had managed to invade the Baltic countries and take Smolensko. The Führer was sure that victory was his.

Despite this discouraging news, nothing could prevent Churchill from determinedly following his plans for achieving total victory over the enemy. During the past few months his relationship with Roosevelt, maintained by letters and telephone calls, had begun to take on a friendlier tone, and Roosevelt went so far as to tell Churchill that he wanted to go to Moscow and meet the English Prime Minister there for a conference with Stalin.

The Atlantic Charter

Indeed, this conference was held in secret, but not in Moscow, rather aboard the American cruiser the *Augusta*, in the waters off Newfoundland, where the draft of an important document christened the Atlantic Charter was agreed upon, consisting of eight points:

— The renunciation of any spirit of conquest.
— There would be no territorial changes without the consent of the people affected.

134

- Total freedom for people to choose their own form of government.
- Free access to all sources of raw materials.
- World economic co-operation.
- Establishment of a peace treaty to ensure the security of all people.
- Open sea routes.
- Total renunciation of the use of force and a policy of disarmament.

Obviously, the Atlantic Charter was not the solution to the armed conflict but only a declaration, but from then on Churchill devoted himself to helping the new ally, the Soviet Union.

A joint operation was quickly prepared. On 25th July the Soviet army invaded Persia from the north, while the English did so from the south and began to seize Abadan. The conquest of Persia resulted in Shah Reza Pahlevi being deported and his son ascending to the throne.

But while this was happening in Persia, developments in Africa were not so favourable. Churchill despaired to see that Rommel was receiving constant reinforcements.

After the disaster at Tobruk, which was conquered by Rommel on 21st June 1942 after eight months of siege, Churchill and his advisors had managed to convince the American president, Roosevelt, and the American army command of North Africa's strategic role. The British, also fearful of losing in Egypt a key piece of its empire and leaving the Near East petroleum route in German hands, had developed the theory of 'attacking the crocodile in its soft underbelly', given the difficulties in 1942 of a landing at the heart of Central Europe. For the London strategists, the 'belly', or weak point, was Italy, and they saw the battles in the Libyan desert as a decisive phase in preparation for an eventual landing in Sicily.

The vital problem from the British standpoint was 'destroying Rommel', and this was the precise order given by Winston Churchill to General Alexander when in August he ordered him to take command of the forces in Egypt and Syria, while upon General Gott's death General Montgomery was sent to command the 8th army, which he first had to reorganise.

The 1942 desert counter-offensive rested on two operations whose strategic objective was to gain control of all of North Africa, ending with the capture of Tunisia, a support point for a landing in the south of Italy. The immense battlefield extended from the Moroccan Atlantic coast to El-Alamein, the last British defence to the advance made by the Afrika Korps between February and July of 1942. In agreement with the Americans, the British government developed the Torch Plan, to which we will refer again, in order to achieve an allied landing in French Africa (Morocco and Algeria) and advance from the west toward the bastions defended by Rommel in Tunisia. From the east, the 8th army was in charge of carrying out Operation Lightfoot to expel Rommel from El-Alamein, Egypt, recover Cyrenaica (Eastern Libya) and conquer Tripoli.

The El-Alamein battle would start off Operation Lightfoot on 23rd October. Sixteen days later, the allies would land at Casablanca and other points along the Moroccan coast in order to begin Operation Torch, which would culminate the same day with the fall of Algiers.

CHAPTER XXIII
JAPAN ATTACKS PEARL HARBOUR

While the coming winter was bringing major problems for the German army in Soviet territory, on 7th December 1941 the Japanese attacked Pearl Harbour. The event had two immediate consequences: first, the United States joined the war, and second, the conflict became virtually worldwide, since a bloody battle began in the Pacific.

As Great Britain would also have to get involved in the conflict with Japan, Churchill saw the need to once again to hold a meeting with President Roosevelt.

Churchill prepared to travel to Washington, and the new conversations began on 22nd December. Churchill spent Christmas at the White House and he attended Congress and went to Canada to deliver several speeches in Ottawa. He then returned to London.

The year 1942 did not begin well. The Japanese invaded Singapore, a British colony. At the same time, the Germans were concentrating their efforts on submarine warfare, attacking the supply ships crossing the Atlantic. In Africa, too, things were not going well for the allies. Supplies for the Afrika Korps had to pass near the coast and by Tobruk, the British beachhead, and Bir-Hakeim, where they had to confront the Free French Light Division. But on 11th June Bir-Hakeim fell after resisting to the limits of its strength.

Churchill once again met with Roosevelt to consider a solution to the requests Stalin was making to the Western allies, since the Soviet dictator asked for a second front to be opened in order to give his army some relief against the Wehrmacht. Churchill then raised the possibility of a landing in North Africa.

During the month of August, the British Premier went to El-Alamein in order to study the situation on the ground. From there he went to Moscow, arriving on 10th August in order to meet with Stalin.

The conversations between Churchill and Stalin lasted five days, since they had totally opposing points of view. Stalin, mistrustful at the beginning, reminded Churchill of his criticisms of Bolshevism and his earlier staunch support for the 'white' army. But these two leaders then devoted themselves to studying strategic problems. Churchill expressed the opinion that he was not in favour of opening a new European front, and he mentioned the fact that an Anglo-American landing would take place in North Africa. Although he was not in agreement, Stalin ended up conceding.

Churchill was once again in Cairo on 16th August, noting with satisfaction that Rommel had not been capable of invading El-Alamein, and that the blockade of Malta had been broken.

Operation Torch

When Churchill returned to London he found that an American general sent by Roosevelt to finalise preparations for Operation Torch was awaiting him. The general was named Dwight Eisenhower.

Churchill no longer doubted that victory was approaching, since the Americans were dealing heavy blows to the Japanese in the Pacific, such that they were gradually re-conquering lost territories. Likewise, on the Russian front the Germans were involved in the terrible battle for Stalingrad, and the

Royal Air Force, supported by the first squadron of the American Eighth Air Force, had finally begun invading German air space.

At the end of October, the offensive against the Afrika Korps began. Alexander and Montgomery valiantly confronted the forces commanded by Rommel, while a powerful Anglo-American fleet was heading toward the North African coasts.

On 8th November the landings in Casablanca, Fedala, Port Lyaytey, Oran and Algeria began. This was what Churchill called 'the end of the beginning', which would obviously lead to the beginning of the end.

Further conversations with Roosevelt

Churchill proposed another conference to Stalin and Roosevelt. Stalin did not accept the invitation, since he claimed that he could not leave the Soviet Union while the bloody battle in the Don basin was underway. Roosevelt did attend, and the meeting was held on 14th January 1943 in Casablanca.

Thanks to Churchill's insistence, De Gaulle, who reached Casablanca on 22nd January, also participated in the conference, as did Giraud. The four men got together to hold the meeting on 23rd January.

This time, Churchill insisted on opening the second European front requested by Stalin, and he also convinced his three cohorts of the need to occupy Tunisia, in order to depart from there to land in Sicily with the aim of invading Italy.

Once the conference was over, after enjoying a day off in Marrakesh, Churchill flew to Cairo and then continued his journey to Istanbul. He tried to get Turkey to declare war against Germany but did not achieve this. He then travelled to Cyprus, where he reviewed his old regiment, the 4th Hussars, and from there he went back to Cairo and then to visit Montgomery in Tripoli.

When he returned to London exhausted, Churchill suffered a bout of pneumonia that left him bedridden for more than three weeks.

But the moment had come which could be defined as the beginning of the end. In spring 1943 the allies stepped up pressure, with the result being the surrender of entrenched enemy troops at the edge of Cape Bon.

On 31st January 1943 the German 6th army under Marshall Von Paulus surrendered in Stalingrad. The Wehrmacht ended up experiencing its greatest defeat since the beginning of hostilities: a catastrophe that proved to be the key moment in the war. After the winter of 1942 to 1943, the Germans never again recovered their offensive power. Their most experienced battalions had been decimated and brought to their knees. The catastrophes experienced on the Russian and African fronts further undermined the people's confidence in the Nazi regimen, especially in their Führer. Germany now realised the fiction of their early victories. When Hitler faced troops as large as his own, he had true strategic problems, and he showed himself for what he really was: a common player whose luck had run out.

On other matters, the Führer continued to ignore all the evidence, incessantly repeating: "I am the only one who has always been right, and no one other than me is capable of directly commanding the German forces".

In Africa the Reich's losses were estimated at a total of one million dead, wounded or taken prisoner, and 8,000 planes, 6,200 guns, 2,500 tanks and 70,000 vehicles destroyed. The initial consequence of the allied victory in Africa, as we shall repeat time and time again, was the assault of Sicily. With this began the invasion of the second pro-Nazi country. The

With Eisenhower in France, in the year 1944.

continental fortress of the Axis would be dismantled at its weakest point.

The coming defeat of Italy would lead to the very heads of the fascist party, with the acquiescence of King Victor Manuel III, joining forces against Mussolini. Il Duce was removed from office and imprisoned. However, a daring German managed to free him and take him to Hitler. The Führer advised him to resist in the north. However, for Mussolini and his political system 'the die had been cast'.

CHAPTER XXIV

THE NORMANDY LANDING

Churchill returned to Washington, but this time not by air but aboard the *Queen Mary*. He was ready to pressure the preparations for Operation Husky, the landing on Sicily, since in his opinion the Americans were dragging their feet in this matter.

Churchill did not leave American soil until he got an official commitment from the American president that the landing in Sicily would be followed by the opening of the Italian front.

Operation Husky began on 10th July. More than five weeks were needed to put an end to German resistance and conquer the island.

Once Sicily was freed, the landing in Italy had to be delayed since Mussolini had been overthrown on 25th July, and based on this incident the German troops had practically flooded Italian territory, such that Churchill had to fly to Quebec in order to meet once again with Roosevelt. The main topic of this new conference was actually the greatest event in World War II, Operation Overlord, better known as the Normandy landing.

The commander assigned to the mission was Eisenhower, and the date agreed upon for the event was 1st May 1944.

On the other hand, in a complementary fashion, Churchill convinced Roosevelt to officially recognise De Gaulle and

Giraud's French committee, which would soon become the provisional government of the French Republic.

In September the landing was made in Salerno, and during the winter of 1943 and the beginning of 1944 the Normandy landing operation was prepared.

In his book *The Second World War*, Churchill would describe this landing in the following way:

> *Our long months of planning and preparations for the greatest maritime operation in history ended on D-Day, 6th June 1944. During the previous night large fleets of convoys with their escorts sailed, completely unknown to the enemy, along the channels previously opened by the minesweepers, from the Isle of Wight to the Normandy coast. The RAF bombers attacked the coastal batteries in their concrete emplacements, dropping five thousand two hundred tonnes of bombs. When day broke, the United States Air Force let itself be seen in order to neutralise the other coastal defences, followed by the medium-range bombers and the fighter-bombers. During the twenty-four hours of that 6th June, the allied air forces made more than fourteen thousand six hundred sorties. Our air superiority was so great that the enemy could only manage a bare one hundred sorties. From midnight on, three air transport divisions landed: the British 6th Air Transport Division north-east of Caen in order to seize the bridgeheads over the river that flows between the city and the sea, and two American air transport divisions whose mission was to support the maritime assault on the beaches north of Carentan and observe the movements of the enemy reserve in order to prevent them from entering the Cotentin peninsula. The objectives were fulfilled.*

When day came and the large and small ships began to occupy their assigned positions for the assault, the scene could almost have been defined as comic. The immediate opposition was limited to an attack made by torpedo launchers which managed to sink a Norwegian destroyer. Even when the naval bombardment began, the reply from the coastal batteries was inconsistent and ineffective. There was no doubt that a surprise attack had been achieved. Numerous landing ships and auxiliary ships full of infantry, tanks, large amounts of munitions and demolition groups of sappers in charge of eradicating coastal obstacles were advancing toward the beach.

The destroyers and rocket launchers and artillery mounted in these landing ships crushed the coastal defences, while at sea, the battleships and cruisers neutralised the fire from the defensive batteries. However, the obstacles and surface and half-hidden mines made the landing hazardous, and many ships were sunk after disembarking their troops. Nonetheless, the advance continued.

As soon as the infantry reached land it headed toward its objectives, and in all cases except one they made notable progress. Our allies sustained extremely violent battle all day, only just to land, and they were not able to open up the way further inland until the 7th. Despite the fact that we had not seized everything we had wanted, especially Caen, which remained in enemy hands, the advances achieved in the first two days of the assault were considered highly satisfactory.

Thus Churchill described the first few hours of the Normandy landing. But the day before D-Day, another memorable event took place which was no less decisive for the allied victory: the occupation of Rome. The following day, Churchill officially announced the news in the House of Commons, while he also informed about the allied landing in Normandy, the famous D-Day.

But what was D-Day? No one knew. One could almost have said: the allies did not know any better than the Germans. The first week of May was coming to an end and a general rehearsal had taken place for the assault forces, but the exact date of the invasion had not yet been set. Eisenhower and Ramsay, the American and the Briton, agreed that it was time to decide. These were the factors in their choice:

1. D-Day had to be a day with strong tides, because with low tides, the obstacles on the beaches were totally uncovered and with high tide, the current would carry the landing ships as high as possible.

2. It was preferable that there should be a moon: this would aid the advance parachutists.

3. D-Day had to be chosen in accordance with H-Hour. H-Hour referred to that moment when the landing craft carrying the first assault wave arrived at the beaches. Once H-Hour was over, the limits of which days could be chosen as D-Day would be specified.

4. H-Hour had to be such that before it there had to be at least sixty minutes of daylight so that the air and naval attacks which would precede the assault could be precise and effective, and the pilots of the landing crafts and vessels heading for the beaches could clearly see in front of and around them.

5. H-Hour had to be chosen such that the sea at that moment was low enough and rising: low enough so that the obstacles were clearly visible, but not so low for the rocks on certain beaches in the British sector to be dangerous, and rising so that during the day two high tides would take place which would allow supplies and provisions to be unloaded more easily.

After studying the pros and cons, Eisenhower decided on 5th June for the Normandy landing.

CHAPTER XXV

THE ATTACK ON LONDON WITH FLYING BOMBS

Nevertheless, despite the advance achieved by the allies in Normandy and Italy, hardships for the British had not yet ended.

Hitler had promised a secret weapon, and it was not long before the first flying bombs were flying over and falling on London. There is nobody better than Churchill himself to describe how those unpiloted rocket-planes worked:

(...) Then the meticulously planned assault on England began by non-guided missiles that were not piloted by human beings. Their objective was Greater London. For more than one year we had argued among ourselves about the nature and scale of the attack, and all the preparations that could be envisioned by our knowledge and allowed by our resources had been made.

In the early hours of 13th June 1944, exactly one week after D-Day, four unpiloted aeroplanes crossed our coasts. They were the premature result of a German order sent urgently on D-Day as a reaction to our success in Normandy. One reached Bethnal Green, where it killed more than six people and injured nine. The others led to no fatalities. Nothing happened again until evening of 15th June, the day on which the Germans began their repressive campaign in earnest. In twenty-four hours, more than two hundred of these missiles were launched against us, and in the following five weeks more than three thousand were to follow.

The flying bomb, as we came to call it, had been christened by Hitler with the name of V-1, since he expected it to be the first in a series of terrifying weapons that were the product of German research. Among the Londoners, the new bombs were known as "buzzbombs", because of the strident tone of their jet engines with a new and ingenious design. The bomb flew at a speed of up to 400 miles per hour at a height of about three thousand feet, and they carried about one tonne of explosives. They were piloted by a compass and a small propeller which, rotated by the air as the bomb moved through the atmosphere, controlled its range. When this propeller had made a certain number of revolutions, corresponding to the distance from the launching base to London, the missile's controls moved, making the bomb go toward the earth. The damage caused by its explosion was enormous, because the bomb usually exploded before reaching the ground.

Later on, in the work from which the previous excerpt was taken, *The Second World War*, Churchill gives an extensive account of the destruction wrought by that lethal weapon:

... As the days went by, all the districts in London were being hit. The greatest damage was caused in a belt extending from Stepney and Poplar towards the south-west to Wandsworth and Mitcham. The most heavily hit district was Croydon, with eight bombs in

a single day, followed by Lewisham, Camberwell, Woolwich and Greenwich, Beckenham, Lambeth, Orpington, Coulsdon and Purley, West Ham, Chislehurst and Mitcham. Approximately three-quarter of a million homes were hit, twenty-three thousand of which were totally destroyed. Yet despite the fact that London suffered the most, the deaths and damage reached a territory that extended far beyond its limits. Certain areas in Sussex and Kent, commonly known as "bomb avenue" because they were in the flight path of the missiles, also suffered heavy punishment. Although they were all directed toward Tower Bridge in London, the bombs fell in a broad zone that ranged from Hampshire to Suffolk. One of them fell near my house in Westerham, killing, by an unfortunate coincidence, twenty-two homeless children and five adults who were gathered in a shelter they had built in the middle of the forest.

Meanwhile, the battle in France continued to rage. On 23rd June, General Eisenhower recommended that forces be concentrated to offer direct support for the decisive battle of Normandy. However, at the beginning of August, major changes had taken place on the Normandy battlefield, and the allies' impetuous eastward march could begin.

A meeting with Tito

That same August, Churchill decided to travel to Italy to, among other things, meet with Tito, which he did on 12th August.

At this and the following meeting, the head of the Yugoslav partisans expressed his willingness to declare publicly, once the war was over, that he would not introduce Communism into Yugoslavia.

Churchill also met with the president of the Yugoslav Council, Subasic, obtaining from both leaders a commitment that they would combine their respective forces in order to unite the Yugoslav people as a single instrument in the fight against the Germans.

Although Churchill was one hundred percent anti-Communist, he gave Tito his unconditional support, even at the expense of actions not too favourable for the Yugoslav monarchists. In spring 1944, Churchill called King Peter of Yugoslavia and advised him to stop the ministries he was forming in the exiled government and to name the former governor of Croatia, Evan Subasic, as head of the new cabinet so that he could lead the negotiations with Tito.

At first the monarch refused Churchill's imposition, since he demanded that Mihajlovic not be part of the new government. However, Churchill remained inflexible and on the following day, without even waiting for the King's reply, he appeared before the House of Commons and declared that Subasic had been entrusted with forming a new Yugoslavian government and that Mihajlovic had thus been deprived of the Defence portfolio.

Meanwhile, on 15th August 1944, the allies landed on the French Mediterranean coast between Marseilles and Nice. On the 24th, the city of Paris celebrated the withdrawal of the Germans. And on 12th September, part of the American army crossed the German border near Eupen, while another contingent of soldiers did the same at Trier. Nonetheless, the Nazis remained steadfast in their defences on the western front and checked the allied advance.

Conversing with President Roosevelt at Yalta.

The Yalta Conference

Between 17th and 26th September, General Montgomery attempted to attack the flank of the Atlantic front via the Dutch plain, but the operation failed due to the difficulties with the terrain.

Churchill was worried: while the allies were advancing slowly in Europe, the Soviet Union's army had reached the Baltic, and Tito was winning in Yugoslavia.

In October, Churchill spent one week in Moscow attempting to find out Stalin's plans. There, a pre-agreement was reached on the destinies of the liberated nations, in which the United States' role was in no way compromised.

However, months later, specifically on 3rd February 1945, a conference was held at Yalta, which was attended by Churchill, Roosevelt, then seriously ill, and Stalin.

The first thing discussed was Germany itself, and the three statesmen defined their respective occupation zones. Churchill managed to get a fourth zone designated for France, against Stalin's claims that France had not fought enough.

Stalin accepted the declaration of war against Japan, making numerous concessions by the United States in the Far East a condition, such as that when the war in Poland ended, it should become a Russian satellite state. In fact, the conference was a triumph for Stalin, but at Yalta another conference was convened for San Francisco, and this would make the people forget that Stalin had been the great victor.

CHAPTER XXVI

THE END OF THE WAR

The end of the war in Europe was approaching.

While the last battles were being fought in Germany, Churchill remained concerned about Soviet expansion. The majority of his telegrams and letters to Roosevelt expressed this, and almost all of the responses from the American president were reassuring.

Roosevelt died on 12th April 1945. Now, Churchill would have to end the war with Truman, the new President of the United States.

On 28th April, Mussolini was taken prisoner and executed. On the 30th of the same month, Hitler committed suicide along with Eva Braun in the Reich Chancellery bunker.

On 1st May the Wehrmacht surrendered on the Italian front, and on the following day the Russians entered Berlin. On the 3rd, the English entered Hamburg and on the 6th, on behalf of the great Admiral Doenitz, Hitler's successor in the Reich, General Jold requested the conditions for surrender.

There were no such conditions for capitulation. On 7th May the Germans signed an unconditional surrender at Rheims.

Churchill gave a radio speech on the 8th. His tone was austere, since he had to warn that the war was not totally over. Japan still had to be defeated.

> *Five years ago I predicted painful and harsh trials; the English people did not give in. I would not*

*consider myself worthy of your trust and your mag-
nanimity if now I did not tell you: Move forward! Be
strong and indomitable until the work is finished and
security and honesty reign all over the world!*

*On the European continent, it remains to be seen
whether the honourable reasons for which we have
participated in a cruel war will not be forgotten: if
the words freedom, democracy and liberation are not
interpreted with very different meanings than the ones
we give them. It would be in vain to punish the
Hitlerites for their crimes if the reign of justice and
law were not established, and if certain totalitarian
governments and police states occupied the place of
the German invaders.*

These last words, as may be imagined, made a clear allu-
sion to the Soviet regime.

When Churchill finished recording this radio message, he
went to the House of Commons, but not without difficulties,
since the crowds poured into the streets in order to celebrate
the victory.

Then a civic procession was planned, starting from Saint
Margaret's Church, where Churchill, the members of the government and the MPs attended a thanksgiving service.

That day, Churchill did not have his wife, Clementine, at
his side. She was in Moscow, where she was making a speech
over the radio to the Soviet people on her husband's behalf.

But the victory in World War II made Churchill face a
strictly democratic problem. The national conciliation government had more than succeeded in the mission for which
it had been formed. Thus, new elections would have to be
called. And Churchill would be unpleasantly surprised.

CHAPTER XXVII
THE POST-WAR IN EUROPE

Churchill had done well to remind the English people that the war was not completely over, since there was still one country fighting: Japan.

However, in Europe the post-war began on 8th May 1945.

Churchill, completely absorbed by the course of the war, had somewhat ignored his country's internal situation. In any case, the British people had behaved in an exemplary fashion during the years of war by resisting the blows the German had given them first by their V-1s, and then by their V-2s. They had also stoically withstood deprivations and rationing.

The same had taken place within the government. The Labour party had dutifully supported the Prime Minister; one could truly say that there had been no more loyal supporter than the Deputy Prime Minister, Clement Attlee, leader of the Labour party.

But in 1944, after the Normandy landing, Churchill had already announced that there would be elections as soon as victory over Hitler was declared.

However, hostilities were not yet completely over, and Churchill wrote this to Attlee, indicating that the best course was to wait until the battle in the Far East was over.

But Attlee, or more accurately, the Labour party, had already taken its decision and immediately submitted the resignation of all Labour party ministers.

This was a harsh blow for Churchill. He had to present his resignation to King George VI, who asked the recently-resigned Prime Minister to form a transition government until elections, which were set for 5th July.

Churchill then confined himself to choosing replacements for the ministers who had stepped down and established a clearly Conservative government.

With the provisional government formed, he once again devoted himself to international matters. He thought a new summit should be held between the three main victorious powers, since not only was Eastern Europe being flooded by Communists, but in compliance with the agreements from the Yalta Conference, the Americans had to leave a major part of conquered Germany to the Soviet Union, thus enlarging the territory separating the Western allies in Poland, making its freedom harder and harder to defend.

The conference was set for 15th July, and it was to be held in Berlin.

As expected, on 15th June the House of Commons was dissolved, and the English people were called to the polls on 5th July. But that vote was different from previous ones: since many voters were still in the services, it was decided that voting should take place all over the world, and the final count was set for 26th July.

The Potsdam Conference

It was finally decided that the conference to be held in Berlin should take place at Potsdam, where it did indeed take place on 17th July.

Churchill was not satisfied with the decisions taken at that conference. Poland was definitively turned into a USSR satellite country, and the territorial claims granted were not really anything more than gains for the Soviets. Churchill had to resign himself to accepting the Oder-Neisse line as the new border between Poland and Germany. The Iron Curtain was inevitably advancing towards the West.

Truman expressed his concern for the end of the aggression, and he appeared to be willing to make major concessions to Stalin in Europe in order to win his support for the war against Japan. Churchill thought that the American president was not making sound decisions, since the help he was requesting from the USSR meant inviting this country to share the glory for a victory it had not made a great contribution. However, at Potsdam, Truman showed himself to be a politician who knew how to take major decisions at the right time. Churchill was duly impressed by the speed with which the president assimilated problems that were completely new to him, and the precise and even rather brusque way he tried to get Stalin to understand that the Western allies were as capable as he was of using violence.

At the Potsdam Conference, Truman revealed to the allies that the atom bomb was ready to be launched against Japan. The idea did not go down well with Churchill, but he decided that not taking that measure and possibly letting the war run its natural course would lead to as many or more deaths than those that would be caused amongst the Japanese by the atom bomb.

Stalin, for his part, did not consider these matters. For him, the issue was clear: if such a weapon was available for finishing off the Japanese, there was no doubt that it had to be used.

On 25th July, the Potsdam Conference met once again. Once the meeting was over, Churchill immediately went to London in order to find out the results of the elections.

The Conference at Potsdam would end the series of allied conferences that laid down the general lines of action once the Axis powers had been defeated, and the much sought peace was achieved. Recapitulating, these conferences were held in Cairo (November 1943), Tehran (28-29th November 1943),

Yalta (February 1945) and Potsdam. At all of them, Churchill played an important role, attempting to keep close tabs on the "red" ally, who was soon to emerge as a rival just as dangerous as the one that had been defeated. Hence the British efforts to establish a future barrier to the USSR in the Balkans. The outcome of the question of Poland, whose government was in exile in London, was a thorn deeply embedded in the side of British statesman, which Churchill never learned to accept.

In fact, the extension of the famous Conference began on 28th July, with Attlee as the Premier substituting for Churchill, and Bevin instead of Eden as the holder of the British Foreign Ministry portfolio. In order to develop the peace treaties with Germany and its satellites, a Council of Foreign Ministers was set up, consisting of the foreign secretaries of the U.S.A., Great Britain, France and China, which would shortly be excluded since it had not participated in the capitulation of Germany. Would the allies, just like in 1918 with the Versailles Treaty, repeat the errors that had contributed to having to once again take up arms a little more than twenty years later?

In order to smother any revanchist claims, the division of Germany and its capital, Berlin, into four military occupation zones was stipulated: American, British, French and Soviet. Logically, the Reich's disarmament and demilitarisation had to be completed. The Nazi party would be dissolved and laws enacted by Hitler abolished, and political decentralisation would take place. Since at that time Germany lacked a central government, authority would come from the occupying powers. At Potsdam, the future Nuremberg trials were also planned against the Nazi hierarchy. Finally, in a declaration dated 26th July, the USSR endorsed the Anglo-American ultimatum to Japan, demanding unconditional surrender.

CHAPTER XXVIII

DEFEATED AT THE POLLS

As can be imagined, Churchill expected to win the elections, although he recognised that while his party had been paralysed by the war, his Labour opponents had been growing stronger since they were organised by labour unionists who during the conflict had remained on the home front in the factories.

However, he still imagined that the Conservatives would gain a substantial majority.

Yet the results could not have been more surprising. The Conservatives lost 10 seats, leaving them with only 198, while the Labour party won 240 and thus had a total of 394 seats, a true triumph for them.

Even in Churchill's own constituency, although he was reelected, there were ten thousand four hundred voters who had voted for his Labour opponent.

On 26th July, Churchill spoke to his fellow countrymen for the last time as Prime Minister:

> *Today the decision of the British people has been made known. I have promptly resigned from the office that was conferred on me in more sombre times. I deeply regret that I will not be allowed to finish the job against Japan, but regardless of this the plans still are available, and perhaps the outcome will be sooner than we think. Now, a fresh responsibility falls*

upon the new government, both in the country and in the world at large, and we must all trust that it will know how to duly assume this. I only wish to express to the British people my deepest and sincerest gratitude for the unyielding support they have given me throughout my painful task, and for all the tokens of affection they have shown me.

The British people's decision logically produced surprise around the world. But that decision, which was so negative for Churchill, in no way meant that the British people would reject the man who had conducted himself so nobly during those terrible moments of the war.

The British had unfailingly followed their Prime Minister. He had brought them victory and had won. However, whilst bitter battles were being waged on the front, people continued to think and assess how the post-war years should be. They had decided that the traditional methods of governing had become obsolete and that a completely new society had to be constructed.

Finally, on 6th August, after sending an ultimatum to the Japanese that had been ignored, the Americans dropped the first atom bomb on Hiroshima, and the second on the 9th on Nagasaki.

On 2nd September the Japanese armed forces surrendered. The capitulation was signed aboard the American battleship *Missouri*.

Mistrust among the allies

After the defeat of Germany and finally Japan, the United States, Great Britain and the Soviet Union only partially reduced their military arsenals. They kept powerful armies

Yalta Conference in February 1945.

on the alert and a considerable arms industry, and continued their feverish searches for new weapons.

By 1945, the world was profoundly divided into two blocks that shared danger had brought together for some time, but which were separated by differences in economic and social structures, as well as by passion and interests. The old system of multilateral balance, centred in Europe, was replaced by a bilateral system of two non-European 'super powers': the United States and the Soviet Union. The Soviet victory, and the institution of 'people's' democracies in Eastern and Central Europe enlarged the 'Communist world' considerably.

From 1943 onward, the prestige gained from the Soviet victories, the affirmation of a military power and the solidity of the regime whose weakness had been denounced for thirty years, constituted a terrible blow for the old society and a source of uneasiness for the Anglo-Saxon powers. Winston Churchill had gone to great lengths to direct the second front requested by Stalin towards 'the soft belly of Europe' – the Danube valley – and to advise Eisenhower and Roosevelt to try and reach Berlin before the Soviets. We must also bear in mind Churchill's benevolence and consideration towards conservative governments and personalities and his fervent anti-Communism. With hindsight we may draw the conclusion that even before the war was over trust between the allies was far from absolute. The economic and political hegemony that the United States planned to exercise was thus limited and disputed from 1945 onward, at a time when the desires for profound reform that had encouraged resistance in all countries terrified the ruling classes and caused them to adhere to the American position.

When operations in Europe and Asia ended, the mistrust on both sides was aggravated, and misunderstandings, suspicions and complaints started to accumulate: the opposition

164

between the allies hardened. As the years went by it began to become a conflict that in all respects – with the exception of actual fighting – came to resemble a veritable war: the Cold War, accompanied by a spectacular reversal of alliances, the defining feature of the post-World War II era. The rivalry between the two largest powers on the planet brought with it a widening of the divisions within each country: enemies and supporters of two views of the world began to face off.

The founding of the United Nations

The gradual disintegration of the alliance was quite rapid. In order to replace the Society of Nations, which had shown itself to be incapable of stopping the war, the three great powers had decided in Yalta to create a new international organisation whose constitution was laid down at the San Francisco Conference that same year, 1945, in the 'United Nations Charter'. Its objective was not only to keep international peace and security, but also to establish world-wide co-operation that would oblige the fundamental freedoms of men to be respected without discrimination and stimulate social progress: *Along with a general assembly that is only consultative in nature, the essential body is the Security Council, which is elected by the assembly. This is subject to the exclusive authority of the great powers, since of the eleven members, five are permanent members (United States, Great Britain, France, China and the Soviet Union), and each of them has the right to veto. The UN will also have an Economic and Social Council with authority over many bodies, including UNESCO, an international court of justice and a secretariat.*

The setback at the polls was a harsh blow for Winston Churchill. For some time he was upset, and in fact, he was justified. At the age of seventy-two and in just a few hours he had gone from being the maximum authority of Great

Britain to being an almost plain citizen without the least responsibility.

Clementine tried to console him as best she could. She even went so far as to say that that defeat might even be a blessing in disguise for him. But Churchill never wanted to be either a hero or a martyr.

He rejected the title of Lord that was offered him. Accepting it would have meant that he could have sat in the House of Lords and he could have ended his days peacefully surrounded by general veneration. But Churchill did not want this. Accepting the title would have also meant abandoning the House of Commons and thus leaving political combat. Obviously, the energetic older man was not willing to stop fighting. During his lifetime he had suffered other setbacks and had managed to overcome them, just as now he would know how to overcome the toughest one of all.

Thus, since he had been re-elected by his constituency, he kept his seat as an MP, and he sat in the first seat on the opposition front bench, as the leader of the Conservatives, a position that was unanimously given to him.

However, before taking on his role as head of the opposition, Churchill, at the recommendation of his personal physician, Lord Moran, took a short break.

The feverish activity during the war was not what had exhausted him. Or perhaps it had, but when he truly realised that he needed a short rest was after the general elections.

When he returned from Italy, the place chosen for his holidays, from his seat as opposition leader Churchill devoted himself to observing the efforts the Labour government was making to solve the serious problems of the post-war. Among other reasons, they had been elected by the voters based on their programme, christened the Welfare Society, but now they realised that they would have to go through several years of deprivation before achieving this ideal. Thus, just as in the

166

first period between the wars, the country's finances devastated by the conflict had had to be restored, the same task was faced then.

The Labour unionists were gradually putting into practice their programme of economic and social reforms, and as of 1946 they nationalised the Bank of England, the coal mines, gas and electricity, the railways and civil aviation.

But the most serious problem faced by the Labour party was maintaining the integrity of the pound sterling. In 1949, the gold and dollar reserves had diminished to such an extent that the currency had to be devalued.

In all the parliamentary debates, Churchill led his party's confrontations with the Government systematically but not always wisely, since he was a man of war and not an economist. Precisely for this reason he was always concerned about putting obstacles in the way of the Government and his speeches never ceased to adopt a rather sarcastic tone.

In the month of September 1949, after a trip to the United States, Churchill found that the Chancellor of the Exchequer had announced a devaluation of the pound sterling. The opposition leader immediately accused the Government of negligence in its functions and demanded that it resign.

However, Attlee did not convene new elections until February of the following year. The outcome of the elections was to give the Labour Party a majority, although it was considerably weakened. Churchill was also returned by his constituency, and he remained at the helm of the opposition.

During 1950 a grave international crisis broke with the outbreak of the Korean War, and everyone believed that a Third World War was about to begin. Likewise, the balance of trade was notably skewed and strikes once again appeared everywhere.

167

In October, Parliament was dissolved and the English had to return to the polls. This time, the Conservatives won. Winston Churchill was asked by the King to form a new government. He would serve as Prime Minister for three more years.

Churchill once again went to work at the helm of the government, in which he named Anthony Eden Minister of Foreign Affairs. He wanted to draw closer to the United States in order to obtain economic aid, and he travelled to Washington repeatedly in order to meet with Truman. Eden always travelled with the Prime Minister. The outcome was not always what Churchill wanted, but on all his trips he managed to reach numerous agreements which could be viewed as advantageous for England.

In the month of February 1952 George VI died. His daughter, Elizabeth Alexandra Mary Windsor, the wife of Prince Philip, Duke of Edinburgh, succeeded him to the throne. She reigned as Elizabeth II, and the people welcomed her warmly.

However, not even the charming Queen Elizabeth II could work the miracle of remedying the difficult situation England was experiencing in 1952 in the twinkling of an eye.

Churchill was obliged to maintain an austere economic policy. Nor could he stop the pace of decolonisation, as much as he would have like to.

Thus 1953 arrived, the year when Elizabeth II decided to name Winston Churchill Knight of the Order of the Garter, which gave him the title of Sir.

That was the homage offered by the Queen, but it symbolised recognition on behalf of the entire English people. Yet it would not be Churchill's only honour that year, since on 16th October the Swedish Academy awarded him the Nobel Prize for Literature. Churchill did not go to the awards ceremony, which was held on 10th December, since that day he was in Bermuda attending a conference.

On 30th November 1954, Churchill turned eighty years old. His birthday celebrations were held at his home among his family, and they ended with a ceremony in the Great Hall at Westminster. The members of the House of Commons gave him the gift of a great portrait of himself that they unveiled at the Westminster reception.

Churchill knew that it was time to retire. He presented his resignation to the Queen on 4th April 1955. That was the last day Churchill resided at 10 Downing Street. But he did not yet entirely retire from politics. He remained an MP until 1964.

CHAPTER XXIX

THE END OF A LONG LIFE

From the end of the war until the end of his life, Churchill spent much more time with his family, especially during the time when he acted as opposition leader and later when he presented his resignation as Prime Minister.

His children visited him often. He had had five, but the family had suffered the misfortune of losing Marigold in 1921, when the girl was only three years old.

Diana had married a Conservative MP, who had a brilliant future. His eldest daughter's husband was named Duncan Sandys, and the couple had given Winston and Clementine Churchill three grandchildren, Julian, Echvina and little Celia.

For his part, Randolph, who would later write a lengthy and brilliant biography of his father, had also married and had increased the family with two more children, Winston and Arabella.

Sarah, the child who had been born at the beginning of World War I, was considered the black sheep of the family. She had devoted herself to dance, in the company of other young people, and in 1936 she ran away from home to marry a young American actor, Vic Olivier. She had divorced him four years later and joined the army during World War II, just like her three brothers and sisters.

Churchill's fourth child was named Mary, and she was possibly the favourite since she was the youngest, having been born in 1929. In 1945, she was twenty-six years old. At that time she was engaged to a young MP who would later serve as Minister of Agriculture, Ambassador in Paris, and would reach the position of Vice-President of the European Community Commission in 1973.

The years from the end of the war until Churchill's death were spent happily in his family home. The old lion's numerous friends were always received with open arms. Perhaps Anthony Eden, who upon Churchill's resignation in 1955 became Prime Minister, was the person who most often visited.

At that time, Churchill devoted himself to writing his memories of World War II, which were still fresh. These were his memoirs of the war, and all the publishing houses vied to publish them. At that time he also considered how to end his great work, *A History of the English-Speaking Peoples.* Sitting on his bed, as he had been doing for some time, both when he wrote and when he took care of affairs in the different ministries, with his cigars and liqueurs at hand, he indefatigably dictated to his secretaries. Between 1948 and 1959, the volumes were published at regular intervals of one to two years. Some excerpts were previously published in newspapers all over the world.

In addition to his literary activities, he continued to wield a bricklayer's trowel and reformed the gardens at Chartwell. He also regularly painted and congratulated Clementine for the good idea she had in 1915 of giving him a beginner's paint box. She told him that from that moment on, his enthusiasm for painting had grown, and whenever he travelled he never forgot his painting gear.

On the matter of painting, Churchill himself wrote:

> *I had turned forty without ever having handled a paintbrush or making my first few marks with a pencil. Nor had I viewed painting all types of pictures as*

With Truman and Stalin at Potsdam (July 1945).

173

a mystery until then, nor had I stood gape-mouthed before at the plaster of pavers only to suddenly find myself immersed in a new and intense form of interest and action, with colours, palettes and canvases without being discouraged by the results... Truly, once I tried it, I realised that it is an amazing experience.

(...)

Now I will tell about my personal experience. When I left the Admiralty at the end of May 1915, I was just another member of the government and the War Cabinet. In this position, I knew everything but could do nothing. My veins were about to burst with the enormous difference of pressures. I had to limit myself to watching how great opportunities were unfortunately passed by, and the timidity with which plans that I myself had conceived and in which I firmly believed were implemented.

That was when the Museum of Painting came to my aid, no doubt not for reasons of charity or gallantry, because after all it had nothing to do with me, and it said:

Some sketches made on a Saturday in the country with my children's paintbox led me to get a complete oil painting set the following morning.

(...) Now I like to paint, even on gloomy days. But in my ardent beginning I demanded sunlight. It was suggested that I visit Avignon because of its admirable light, and there is certainly no place more delightful for an aspiring painter. Then Egypt, violent and brilliant, presenting infinite variations on its threefold subjects: the Nile, the desert and the sun. Or Palestine, land of rare beauty that deserves a true artist's attention. And what can be said about India? Who has ever rendered its squalid splendour? But after all, *with only the sun trying to shine, one does not need to venture further than one's one country. There is nothing more intense than the burnished steel and gold of a Scottish brook in the highlands; and almost every day at dawn and sunset, the Thames provides Londoners with glories and delights for which one has to travel far to find a rival.*

Since he had a steady income from his literary activities, he was able to buy some race horses, one of which, *Columnist*, won several prizes that satisfied his owner.

Toward the end of a long life

After he resigned as Prime Minister, Winston Churchill's health began to decline.

Each year, Churchill awaited the arrival of winter to leave London and head for Marrakesh, where he was comforted by the African sun.

Onassis, with whom he was quite close, made an aeroplane available to Churchill so he could travel to North Africa in comfort. The Greek shipowner almost always accompanied him personally.

When he returned to his estate, Chartwell, or during the time he spent in London attending Parliamentary sessions, Clementine made sure that there was always a dinner guest, since Churchill enjoyed company.

In November 1959, when he returned from breakfast with Lord Beaverbrook, Churchill suffered an attack, collapsing on the seat of his Rolls-Royce. However, he managed to recover, although he gradually had to give up his artistic and literary pursuits.

In 1964 new elections were called in Great Britain. The elderly Winston Churchill was never again to run.

On 15th January 1965, Churchill suffered from a stroke that left him in a deep coma from which he would never awaken. On 24th January, precisely seventy years after his father had died, by a coincidence of fate, Churchill drew his last breath.

There were ten people around him: six family members, Doctor Moran, Mr Montagne Brown, Nurse Huddlestone and his nurse and aid Roy Howells.

His funeral was set for six days later. In London, flags flew at half mast and the funeral cortège paraded from Westminster through Trafalgar Square and Fleet Street to Saint Paul's Cathedral, where his funeral rites were performed. There the Queen and her family, the entire Government and numerous foreign heads of state awaited him.

His remains were covered with the Union Jack. When the funeral service was over, the coffin was taken aboard a motor boat that sailed along the Thames as far as Waterloo Station, from where a special train set off for Blenheim, where he was to be buried.

CHRONOLOGY

1874 — Winston Churchill is born on 30th November at Blenheim Palace, the home of his grandfather, the 7th Duke of Marlborough.
    — On 27th December he is baptised with the names Winston Leonard Spencer Churchill.

1877 — Lord Randolph Churchill, Winston's father, moves his family to Ireland in order to work with his father, the Viceroy of Ireland.

1880 — His brother, Jack, is born in February.
    — The family returns to London in March and moves into the mansion at Saint James' Place.

1881 — In November he begins at the St. George Preparatory School, at Ascot, where he will remain as a boarder until 1884.

1886 — Winston Churchill suffers a serious bout of pneumonia, from which he almost dies.

1887 — He attends Harrow Public School.

1888 — Guided by his father, he chooses a military career, and his studies prepare him for the Sandhurst Military Academy entrance examination.

1890 — He sits for the Sandhurst entrance examination for the first time, and does not pass.

1893 — He finally passes the examination in June, after having failed in the month of January. He is ranked 95th out of 389 candidates, although he needs a recommendation in order to be accepted, since his grade is not high enough.

1895 — He leaves the Military Academy with the rank of Second Lieutenant.
— The same year, his father dies on 24th January.
— He is sent to the 4th Hussars in Aldershot.
— He sets out as an observer for Cuba, where the Spanish are facing a dangerous insurrection.

1896 — In the month of September, his regiment is moved to Bangalore, India.

1897 — He witnesses the campaign against the insurrection of the native Pathans as the correspondent for the magazine *Pioneer* from Allahabad and the *Daily Telegraph* of London.
— He publishes *The Malakand Field Force*, in which he recounts the campaign against the Pathans.
— In barely two months, he writes his first novel, *Savrola*.

1898 — He participates in the conquest of the Sudan with the 21st Lancers.
— He is promoted to the rank of Lieutenant.
— He writes *The River War*.

1899 — Back in London, he runs for elections for the first time in the Oldham constituency and is defeated.

— He is named war correspondent for the *Morning Post* and leaves for South Africa to participate in the Boer War. He is taken prisoner and manages to escape.

1900 — He once again runs in Oldham with the Conservative party. He wins his first parliamentary seat.

— He writes two books on the Boer War.

1904 — In a rather spectacular move, he breaks with the Conservatives and becomes a Liberal on 31st May.

1905 — He occupies his first public office when he is appointed Under-Secretary of the Colonial Office.

1906 — He presents his Liberal candidacy for the constituency of Manchester. He wins the seat by a considerable majority.

— The biography of his father, Lord Randolph, is published.

1907 — He writes a book on a trip taken in east Africa: *My Africa Journey*.

1908 — On 12th April he begins a relationship with his future wife, Clementine Hozier.

— He is offered the Ministry of Trade but is beaten in Manchester north-east by a rival Conservative, although he later runs for Dundee and achieves a sweeping victory, so he can accept the portfolio.

— On 12th September he weds Clementine.

1909 — His first child, christened Diana, is born on 11th July.

1910 — He is re-elected for the Dundee district.
— He is appointed Home Minister.

1911 — As Home Minister, he directs the assault against an old house on Sidney Street in which anarchists had taken refuge during disturbances.
— His son, Randolph, is born on 28th May.
— In October he is named Minister of the Navy and is thus given the post of First Lord of the Admiralty.

1914 — World War I breaks out in June. The English fleet, thanks to Churchill's competent administration, is prepared for the event.
— His daughter, Sarah, is born.

1915 — In April, the English are defeated at Gallipoli, and Churchill is somehow blamed for the failure.
— After leaving his duties, Churchill presents himself to the commander of the English troops in France as a common soldier.

1916 — Thanks to a favourable report from the Investigating Commission of the Dardanelles expedition, Churchill returns to active politics and is named new Minister for Armament and Munitions.

1918 — His daughter, Marigold, is born.
— The war ends and Churchill is made Minister of War.

1919 — His daughter, Mary, is born.

Churchill's investiture in the Order of the Garter, April 1952.

1921 — He is changed from Minister of War to Minister of the Colonies.
— Ireland's independence is consummated.
— He meets Lawrence of Arabia.
— His daughter, Marigold, suddenly dies.

1922 — He is left with neither a ministry nor a seat in the House of Commons.
— He devotes himself to resting for a time on the Riviera, where he paints and writes *The World Crisis*.
— He exhibits his paintings at a Paris gallery under a pseudonym.

1924 — Churchill becomes a Conservative once again, taking advantage of the Liberals' weakness.
— After running in Leicester in 1923 for the Liberals, in October 1924 he runs in Epping and is easily elected.
— He is named Chancellor of the Exchequer.

1926 — He attempts to correct the balance of payments by a reduction in salaries and has to face a nine-day general strike.
— At the new elections for the House of Commons, he is returned, but he does not form not part of the Government, which is dominated by the Labour party.
— He writes *My Early Life*.

1932 — In order to write a biography of his ancestor, the first Duke of Marlborough, he travels to Germany and there takes note of the rise of Nazism as espoused by Adolf Hitler.
— Back in England, Churchill gives a speech in the House of Commons in which he warns of the danger Hitler poses.

1933 — Hitler gains power in Germany. Churchill continues to warn about the danger and in the House of Commons explains that the Nazi German Luftwaffe has a force on a par with Great Britain's.

1935 — The Conservatives regain the majority in the House of Commons. However, Churchill has no portfolio, although he is returned by the Epping constituency.

1936 — On 20th January, King George V dies. The Prince of Wales, Churchill's friend, who reigns under the name of Edward VIII, succeeds him on the throne, but he abdicates in favour of George VI after three hundred days.
— The Spanish Civil War begins.
— The Rhineland invasion begins in France.

1937 — On 17th May the new king, George VI, is crowned. Churchill cannot attend the ceremony because he holds no public office other than that of Member of Parliament.
— He publishes the biography of his ancestor, the first Duke of Marlborough.

1939 — On 1st September Hitler invades Poland. On 3rd September France and England declare war on Germany.
— Chamberlain, the English Prime Minister, forms a War Cabinet in which Churchill serves as First Lord of the Admiralty.

1940 — On 8th May, Chamberlain resigns and the King asks Churchill to form a new government, of which he will be Prime Minister and Minister of Defence.

1941 — On 11th July Churchill signs an agreement with the Soviet representative in which Great Britain and the USSR agree not to negotiate a separate peace.

— On 24th August Churchill and Roosevelt sign the Atlantic Charter on the American cruiser, the *Augusta*.

— On 7th December the Japanese attack Pearl Harbour and the United States declares war on Japan.

1942 — Churchill meets with Stalin for the first time.

1943 — In the month of January, Churchill meets Roosevelt, De Gaulle and Giraud in Casablanca. Stalin declines the invitation.

— After occupying Tunisia, the allies open a second front on Sicily, in order to invade Italy.

— In November, Churchill, Roosevelt and Stalin meet in Tehran.

1944 — The Normandy landing takes place on 6th June.

1945 — The Yalta Conference is held in February on the Crimean peninsula, which would close with a major Soviet victory.

— On 17th May German troops surrender.

— Churchill gives a speech in the House of Commons in which he warns that the war was not yet over: Japan had yet to be defeated.

— On 25th June Churchill is defeated at the polls after attending the Potsdam Conference, where he held talks on Europe's destiny. The Soviet Union once again is the victor.

Meeting with Montgomery in 1964, recalling the difficult years of World War II.

185

1945 — On 6th August the USA drops the first atom bomb on Hiroshima, and on the 9th of the same month the Japanese sign the armistice on board the American battleship, the *Missouri*.

— Churchill devotes himself to writing *The Second World War*. He also resigns from his post as opposition leader.

1950 — After the October elections, in which the Conservatives prevail, Churchill forms a new government and is once again Prime Minister of Great Britain.

1953 — By conferring on Churchill the title of Knight of the Order of the Garter, Elizabeth II names him Sir.

— He wins the Nobel Prize for Literature.

— He suffers from a minor stroke during a dinner with De Gasperi at Downing Street.

1954 — The Parliament pays him homage in honour of his eightieth birthday.

1955 — He presents his resignation to the Queen and leaves 10 Downing Street after a farewell dinner for Elizabeth II and the Duke of Edinburgh.

— He devotes himself more intensely to travelling, painting and writing.

1956 — He publishes *A History of the English-Speaking Peoples*.

— His health quickly begins to deteriorate.

1958 — He suffers an attack of bronchopneumonia and his literary and parliamentary activities come to a close.

1964 — He does not run for the House of Commons elections and thus retires from public life.

1965 — Early on the morning of 28th January, he dies at his home in Hyde Park Gate.

INDEX